IN MODERN GERMAN

To my friend
Jerry,
with great
apprekiation

NORTH-HOLLAND
LINGUISTIC SERIES 10
Edited by S. C. DIK and J. G. KOOIJ

NOMINALIZATION AND COMPLEMENTATION IN MODERN GERMAN

H. ESAU

College of Liberal Arts
Texas A&M University

1973

NORTH-HOLLAND PUBLISHING COMPANY
AMSTERDAM · LONDON

AMERICAN ELSEVIER PUBLISHING COMPANY, INC.
NEW YORK

Library of Congress Catalog Number 73-88162

North-Holland ISBN for this series 0 7204 6180 4
North-Holland ISBN for this volume 0 7204 6192 8
American Elsevier ISBN 0 444 10584 0

Publishers:
NORTH-HOLLAND PUBLISHING COMPANY – AMSTERDAM
NORTH-HOLLAND PUBLISHING COMPANY, LTD. – LONDON

Sole distributors for the U.S.A.:
AMERICAN ELSEVIER PUBLISHING COMPANY, INC.
52 VANDERBILT AVENUE
NEW YORK, N.Y. 10017

PRINTED IN THE NETHERLANDS

ACKNOWLEDGEMENT

For permission to reprint copyrighted material grateful acknowledgment is made to the following:

Cambridge University Press and Jane Robinson: From 'Case, Category and Configuration' by Jane Robinson, in *Journal of Linguistics* (1969) 6, 57–80. Copyright by Cambridge University Press.

Holt, Rinehart and Winston, Inc. and Charles J. Fillmore: From 'The Case for Case' by Charles J. Fillmore, in E. Bach and R. T. Harms [eds.], *Universals in Linguistic Theory*. Copyright, 1968, by Holt, Rinehart and Winston, Inc.

Mouton & Co.: From 'Order of the Elements in the German Verb Constellation' by Helmut Esau, in *Linguistics* (1973) 98.20–40. Copyright by Mouton & Co. N.V., Publishers, The Hague.

To
Naomi,
Kenny and Penny

PREFACE

The last few years have seen a number of syntactic descriptions of modern German, some of which treat identical phenomena. Every new investigation sheds some new light on the data and thus brings us closer to the goal of descriptive adequacy. But every new description also forces us to account for more and more unexplained facts. It is precisely this uncovering process that leads us to a confrontation with theoretical and metatheoretical questions. The present analysis raises a number of such questions which must be taken into account in future descriptions of German.

This work represents the first systematic application of the Case model of grammar to German syntax. The application has led to an adequate accounting of a number of previously unexplained phenomena in German. For example, I have given a description of the *ung*-nominals in chapter 5 by assuming a well-defined semantic class within the lexicon whose members are in part the result of applying the *ung*-derivation to the corresponding verbs.

The real significance of my investigation, however, lies in the insight which it provides into the structure of the lexicon and into the role of semantics. If the conception of lexical structure as set forth in chapter 5 appears a bit simplistic, the reader should keep in mind that the scope and primary purpose of the study prevented a detailed discussion of lexical relationships. I am presently developing this topic in a separate paper.

The second insight, too, which concerns the nature of the semantic component, could not be explored in great depth. Recent discussions concerning the relationship between semantics and syntax have centered primarily around the question whether the base generates syntactic or semantic structures. The discussion in chapters 3 and 5 indicates that the central issue to be resolved should probably be formulated as follows:

Where does the alignment between semantics and syntax occur?

The data considered suggests that semantic-syntactic alignment takes place at two places in the grammar:

(1) The semantic case functions align in a language-specific way with the syntactic deep case phrases and
(2) The primary semantic classes of the lexicon align into the major syntactic categories (Noun, Verb, Adjective, etc.).

A lexical model which conceives of the relationship between primary semantic classes and major syntactic classes as one of semantic-syntactic alignment can explain quite naturally the fact that both the Adjective *happy* and the Noun *sight*, after undergoing certain derivations, can end up in the same syntactic category Adverb as the formatives *unhappily* and *unsightly*.

A few words are necessary to explain the system of numbering used. Sentences used for illustration are numbered consecutively in each chapter. Tree diagrams which illustrate the structure of a sentence under discussion carry the same number as the corresponding sentence preceeded by the letter T in parentheses.

Diagrams and illustrations without corresponding sentences are numbered independently, as Fig (1), etc.

The present form of this work represents an expanded and revised version of my Ph.D. dissertation which was submitted to the University of California, Los Angeles, in 1971.

A subsequent grant from Texas A&M University has helped make possible the modifications which were necessary for its publication.

I am especially grateful to my supervisor, Terence Wilbur, for the many hours of discussion which have resulted in numerous valuable ideas for improvement.

I would like to thank Raimo Anttila, Victoria Fromkin, and Stephen P. Schwartz for their sympathetic and helpful criticism. The study has benefited greatly from discussions with Mervin Barnes, Vera Hogan, Sandra Annear-Thompson, Marianne Celce-Murcia and Johannes G. Kooij who have all read a preliminary version. I am much indebted also to Jerold Edmonson for his many helpful comments which were greatly responsible for the progress of the work. Finally I want to thank Elizabeth Turpin for her help in preparing the manuscript for publication.

CONTENTS

Preface

1. GRAMMATICAL FRAMEWORK

1.1. Preliminary Remarks

My brief survey of traditional treatments of
nominalization in German has led to rather meager
results. It is for this reason among others that I
shall attempt to formalize certain generalizations
about Nominal structures in German. I have adopted a
Generative framework for my analysis since Generative
grammar appears to allow for a more adequate treatment
of nominalization (and, for that matter, of syntactic
structure in general) than any of the linguistic theories
preceding it.

Several versions of Generative grammar have been
proposed during the last decade, some of which modify
Chomsky's Standard Theory[1] considerably. In my
description I shall adhere to a modified version of
Fillmore's Case grammar since I believe this to be the
most adequate theory for an account of German. Of

course, adequacy is an empirical question since there
is no way of deciding a priori which theory will yield
the simplest and most revealing description of the language.
However, it will be necessary to sketch the development
and modifications that the theory of Generative grammar
has undergone, before outlining my position with regard
to the conflicting versions of the theory.

Most of the work involving Nominals has been done
for the English language. A brief appraisal of the major
contributions on English nominalization is, therefore,
not to be avoided and will be given below. Theoretical
questions concerning the treatment of Nominals have
figured heavily in the development of Generative grammar
and led to the proposal of a number of alternative
theories. A general outline of the development of
Generative grammar from its inception by Noam Chomsky
until today will, therefore, include the major
contributions concerning the treatment of Nominals in
the grammar as well.

1.2. Chomsky's model

The publication of Syntactic Structures (1957) marks
the beginning of the development of Generative grammar.
This book introduces the most basic concept of Generative
grammar, namely, that the syntactic component of a

grammar contains a set of context-free base rules and
an ordered set of transformational rules. Syntactic
Structures was superseded in 1965 by Aspects of the
Theory of Syntax, which introduces some essential
modifications, two of which are pertinent for purposes
of our discussion. The first of these is the separation
of the lexicon from the categorial component of the
base and the other is the abolition of the claim that
a syntactic description must be non-semantic, i.e., that
no semantic criteria are to be used in the construction
of a grammar. I shall return to both of these points
when discussing the various hypotheses regarding the
treatment of Nominals.

1.2.1. Chomskian model defined

A grammatical description of a language is made up
of three main parts: a syntactic component, a
phonological component and a semantic component. The
syntactic component of the Aspects model consists of
a set of base rules and a lexicon of all the morphemes
of the language. The phrase structure rules (PSR)
of the base are recursive and constitute the sole
creative part of the syntactic component. The output
of the PSR consists of a string of terminal symbols

which, after lexical insertion, is interpreted as the
deep structure of a sentence. Leaving aside the
semantic component, these deep structures are then
transformed into surface structures by a set of
transformational rules which operate on phrase markers,
i.e., they map basic phrase markers into derived phrase
markers. The Aspects model may be illustrated as
follows:

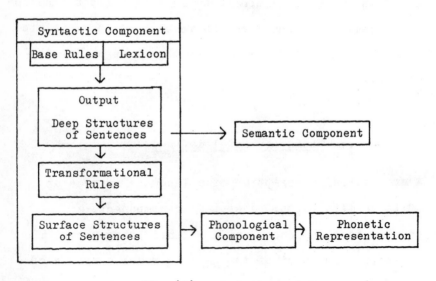

Fig (1): Aspects model

The base rules are a set of context-free rewrite rules
of the form X ⟶ Y (i.e., X is rewritten as Y),[2] as
shown below:

```
S  ────→ NP  VP
VP ────→ V   NP              These rules generate deep
NP ────→ (Det)  (Adj) N      structures of sentences.
      etc.
```

This model claims, in adherence to the Katz-Postal
hypothesis (1964), that all semantic information is
given in the base. This is equivalent to saying that
transformations do not change meaning but are solely
interpretative.

Chomsky tried to avoid the mixing of categorial
notions with relational (functional) ones by asserting
that syntactic relational information (including such
concepts as Subject or Object of the sentence) can be
defined metatheoretically as a set of conditions on
configurations of categories. In other words, the
syntactic notions of Subject and Object are stated in
the metatheory as: (1) Subject is the NP dominated
by S (formally represented as (NP, S)) and (2) Object
is the NP under VP (NP, VP) as follows:

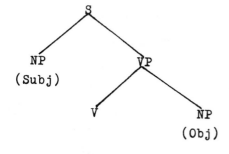

Fig (2): Configuration
defining the relations:
Subject of and Object of

Implicit in Chomsky's approach is the claim that
this information has a function in a competence grammar,
namely that Subject of and Object of are semantically
relevant notions, on which the semantic interpretation
of the sentence depends. (Note that Chomsky's position
means that Subject and Object are deep structure
relations.)

1.3. Fillmore's Deep Case Hypothesis

Fillmore's Case grammar proposal (Case for Case 1968)
came as a reaction to the phrase structure grammar as
advocated by Chomsky in Aspects. He questions whether
or not the semantic notion of Subject is correlated
with the surface Subject. Fillmore shows that in many
instances one cannot give a consistent semantic
interpretation to the concept Subject or Object. This
may be seen from the following sentences:

> (1) Der Mann zerbrach die Scheibe mit dem Ball.
>   (Agent + Verb + Objective + Instrumental)
> (2) Der Ball zerbrach die Scheibe.
>   (Instrumental + Verb + Objective)
> (3) Die Scheibe zerbrach.
>   (Objective + Verb)

As the Object of the action die Scheibe has the same

relationship to the Verb in all three instances.
Assuming for the moment that the meaning of a sentence
can be derived from its deep structure, one would
expect to find this constant semantic relationship
between the NP die Scheibe and its Verb zerbrach
expressed in each instance. However, Chomsky's
configurationally defined deep notions Subject and
Object are unable to reveal this consistent semantic
information, since the NP under S depends in part on
the presence or absence of other elements in the sentence.
The need for stating certain co-occurrence restrictions
between NP's also makes it imperative that semantic
relations be expressed consistently, no matter which
NP will end up as surface Subject of the string. E.g.,
if an inanimate Subject is present, no Instrumental is
permitted. One, therefore, does not get sentences of
the following kind:

(4) *Das Auto zerbrach die Scheibe mit dem Ball.

Only if an animate Agent is realized can we also use an
Instrumental. On the other hand, if the string has no
Agent, the Instrumental can be placed in the Subject
position. It is obviously not sufficient to define the
notions Subject and Object configurationally, as Chomsky
did, since such a definition does not allow for one

particular NP to be interpreted consistently in every
case.

Fillmore states that <u>Subject of</u> is only a surface
notion which is semantically irrelevant. This leads
him to suggest, therefore, that NP under S is not in
the deep structure at all. The semantic interpretation
must be on a deeper level, where all cases are defined
according to <u>Deep Case Functions</u> (i.e., semantic
interpretations given NP's by the base). These are
defined metatheoretically. Depending on which of the
options are in the tree, the string ends up with a
certain surface Object or surface Subject. But these
cannot be configurationally defined at the deepest
level. Fillmore's deep structure for sentence (5)
would then appear as the tree diagram (T5).[3]

(5)   Der Mann zerbrach die Scheibe mit dem Ball.

(T5)

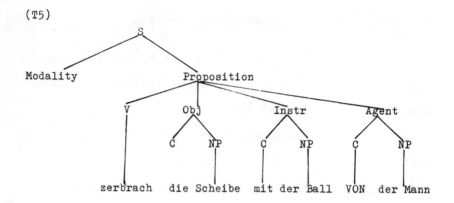

In the deep structure NP's appear under proposition
with their case information. A Subject placement rule
operates later on one of the NP's and puts it immediately
under S. If the Agent is chosen we get the surface
sentence:

(6) Der Mann zerbrach die Scheibe mit dem Ball.

If our option for Subject is the Instrumental, then the
surface sentence (7) is realized:

(7) Der Ball zerbrach die Scheibe.

The metatheoretically defined co-occurrence restrictions
tell us that in the latter case we cannot have an Agent
present. It would, for example, be ungrammatical to say

(8) *Der Ball zerbrach die Scheibe von dem Mann.

No NP as such has the position NP under S in the deep
structure; instead we have a proposition with NP's in
case relations to one another and the Verb. By a later
transformation some NP is always moved into the position
of surface Subject.

The form of Fillmore's Case grammar is the following:

S ⟶ M + P

P ⟶ V + (O)   (D)   (I)   etc.

$\begin{Bmatrix} O \\ D \\ I \end{Bmatrix}$ ⟶ Prep + NP

where M = Modality, P = Proposition, O = Objective,
     D = Dative, and I = Instrumental.

In the lexicon every Verb is marked as insertable in
certain contexts of cases; e.g., zerbrechen
[+ _____ O (I) (A)].

The crucial problem for the Case grammar proposal
is to find a set of universally clear and defined cases
which have a constant semantic interpretation for each
case. The following definitions for cases are given
by Fillmore (1968:24-25):

> 'Agentive (A), the case of the typically animate
> perceived instigator of the action identified by
> the verb.
>
> Instrumental (I), the case of the inanimate force
> or object causally involved in the action or state
> identified by the verb.
>
> Dative (D), the case of the animate being affected

by the state or action identified by the verb.
<u>Locative</u> (L), the case which identifies the
location or spatial orientation of the state or
action identified by the verb.
<u>Objective</u> (O), the semantically most neutral case,
the case of anything representable by a noun whose
role in the action or state identified by the
verb is identified by the semantic interpretation
of the verb itself; conceivably the concept should
be limited to things which are affected by the
action or state identified by the verb. The term
is not to be confused with the notion of direct
object, nor with the name of the surface case
synonymous with accusative'.

1.4. <u>Nominalization</u>

1.4.1. <u>Transformationalist hypothesis</u>

Recent work in English syntax has shown that there are
basically two ways within a Generative framework in
which Nominals can be derived. The earliest extensive
Generative analysis of nominalization is R. Lees' (1960)
<u>The Grammar of English Nominalization</u>. Although Lees
offered some very insightful generalizations, his work
was limited by the fact that it had to operate within

the inadequate framework of <u>Syntactic</u> <u>Structures</u> (Chomsky 1957). At this early date the lexicon was still part of the base categorial component; the base rules for such a simple sentence as <u>Der Mann warf den Ball</u> would look like the following:

(i)   S ⟶ NP + VP

(ii)   NP ⟶ T + N

(iii)   VP ⟶ Verb + NP

(iv)   T ⟶ der

(v)   N ⟶ Mann, Ball

(vi)   Verb ⟶ warf

Within this model of syntactic description, it was natural for Lees to attempt a transformational derivation of deverbal Nouns because it was not possible to express existing relationships in the lexicon. Lees (1960), therefore, proposed that Nominals which are related to Verbs and Adjectives (e.g., <u>propose</u> - <u>proposal</u>; <u>eager</u> - <u>eagerness</u>) be derived from underlying sentences by means of transformations. As Chomsky (1967) points out, it is only since the separation of the lexicon from the categorial component of the base and the analysis in terms of contextual features, which cross-classify, that an alternative approach was provided for.

1.4.2. Lexicalist hypothesis

Chomsky (1968) showed that the weakness of deriving
Nominals like refusal, certainty, proposal, etc.
transformationally are of two kinds: (1) those due
to the varied and idiosyncratic nature of the semantic
relations between derived Nominals and their associated
verbal/adjectival cognates, and (2) those arising from
the unpredictable syntactic properties of Nominals.

With regard to the semantic idiosyncracies consider
the classic examples:

(9a) The president proposed to end the war in
      Viet Nam.

(9b) The president's proposal to end the war in
      Viet Nam ...

(9c) The tradition continued.

(9d) The continuation of the tradition ...

(9e) The continuity of the tradition ...

Sentence (9a) could only be paraphrased as: The president
proposed that the president would end the war; (9b),
however, is ambiguous between Equi-NP-delection, i.e.,
that the president would end the war, and
Indefinite-NP-deletion, i.e., that someone would end
the war. The strings (9d) and (e) are clearly
semantically distinct which again argues against their

derivation from the same proposition.[4]

The syntactic properties of derived Nominals are
also unpredictable from underlying sentential structures
containing a related Verb or Adjective. The following
examples from the UESP grammar (1968:1.4) will illustrate
the problem:

(10a) His enthusiasm is annoying.

(10b) *His enthusiasms are annoying.

(10c) His criticism is annoying.

(10d) His criticisms are annoying.

(10e) His inference was correct.

(10f) His inferences were correct.

(10g) His insistence was emphatic.

(10h) *His insistences were emphatic.

A knowledge of neither the underlying proposition nor
the properties of a particular Nominal affix will help
us predict such noun-like features as [+/-COUNT]. His
inferences is grammatical but *his insistences is not;
these are clearly idiosyncratic properties characteristic
of lexical items.

Derived nominals, according to the UESP grammar
'... behave like nouns in all respects--full range of
determiners, relativization, noun features like
[+/-COUNT] governing pluralization and determiner

selection' (1968:1.4). It is this same group of
Nominals that Chomsky (1967) has shown to be very
restricted along the parameter of productivity.

The following examples are taken from Chomsky
(1967:5):

> (11a) John is easy to please.
>
> (11b) John is certain to win the prize.
>
> (11c) John amused the children with his stories.
>
> (12a) *John's easiness to please ...
>
> (12b) *John's certainty to win the prize ...
>
> (12c) *John's amusement of the children with
>   his stories ...
>
> (13a) John's eagerness to please ...
>
> (13b) John's certainty that Bill will win
>   the prize ...
>
> (13c) John's amusement at the children's
>   antics ...

If a transformational derivation were assumed for examples
(12) and (13), it would not be clear how these restrictions
could be easily stated or adequately explained. On
the other hand, there is a second type of Nominals--
including Infinitives, Gerundives and clausal
types--which do not behave like Nouns to the extent
derived Nominals do in that they exclude relative clauses

and are quite restricted with regard to Determiner
selection, but which are totally productive.

There is general agreement that Infinitives,
Gerundives, and clausal nominalizations in English ought
to be derived transformationally, so that the division
between transformational and lexical derivation would
coincide with the dichotomy productivity vs. restricted
productivity of Nominals. The lexicalist position,
as set forth by Chomsky (1967), proposes to derive
only the totally productive Nominals transformationally
from an underlying proposition containing verbal or
adjectival cognates. All other nominalizations of the
type, <u>certainty</u>, <u>eagerness</u>, <u>proposal</u>, <u>refusal</u>,
<u>construction</u>, ... are only lexically related to their
verbal/adjectival cognates.

1.4.3. <u>X-Bar</u> <u>Convention</u>[5]

One disadvantage of the lexicalist position was its
inability to show the obvious structural similarity
between such strings as (14a) and (14b):

(14a) Der General schlägt vor, den Kampf
       zu beenden.

(14b) Der Vorschlag des Generals, den Kampf
       zu beenden ...

In order to capture the correspondence between the
internal structure of the VP (14a) and the internal
structure of the NP (14b) Chomsky (1967) proposed the
X-Bar convention. He made use of the notions <u>head</u>,
<u>complement</u>, and <u>specifier</u> in order to show the
parallelism between structures whose heads belong to
different lexical categories. He asserted that 'for
any lexical category X, the highest relevant level of
structure, represented by convention as $\bar{\bar{X}}$, incorporated
the immediate constituents specifier-of-$\bar{X}$ and $\bar{X}$, the
latter breaking down into the head, X, and its
complement' (UESP 1968:1.6). The claim was that, no
matter if the head was a V, an N, or an A, the dependent
structures were essentially parallel.

  1.4.4. <u>Fusion</u> <u>of</u> <u>Lexicalist</u> <u>with</u> <u>Deep</u> <u>Case</u>
          <u>hypothesis</u>

The UESP grammar (1.5ff.) points out a number of
difficulties which the X-Bar proposal in its original
form contains and gives examples where the assumed
parellelism breaks down. The strings (15a) and (b)
would under the X-Bar convention correspond to the
structures (T15a) and (b) respectively.

  (15a) Der Feind zerstörte die Stadt.
  (15b) Die Zerstörung der Stadt durch den Feind ...

(T15a)

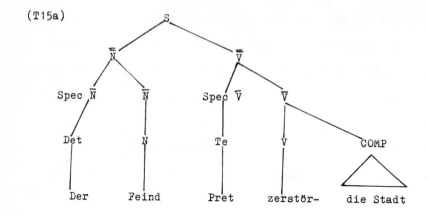

(T15b)

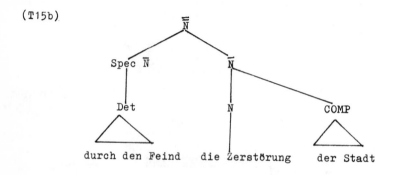

The grammatical relationship between <u>Feind</u> and
<u>zerstörte</u>/<u>Zerstörung</u> is clearly parallel and should
be captured in a descriptively adequate grammar. Yet
<u>der</u> <u>Feind</u> in (T15a) remains outside $\overline{\overline{V}}$, whereas <u>durch</u>
<u>den</u> <u>Feind</u> (T15b) appears under $\overline{\overline{N}}$, within the Spec-of-$\overline{N}$.
The breakdown of the parallelism which the X-Bar
convention attempts to establish is due primarily to
the Subject-Predicate deep structure analysis of the
<u>Aspect</u> model.

To overcome the 'incompatability of the X convention
with a subject-predicate analysis of the sentence' (1.8)
the UESP grammar adopts Fillmore's deep case hypothesis.
We read further that 'since the deep structure based on
cases recognizes no special significance in the subject
of a sentence, or, of course, in a genitive, it is to
that extent well-adapted to the lexicalist hypothesis'
(UESP 1968:1.8).[6] If a deep case base were used,
structures (T15a) and (b) would be represented as
(T15a') and (b'):

(T15a')

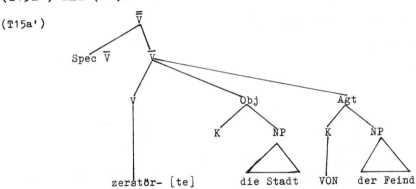

zerstör- [te]   die Stadt   VON   der Feind

(T15b')

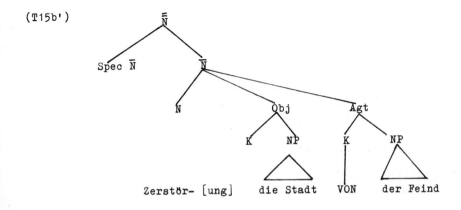

Zerstör- [ung]   die Stadt   VON   der Feind

It is apparent that the adoption of deep cases into
the base yields perfectly parallel structures for the
forms (15a) and (15b); this is essential for the lexicalis
hypothesis.[7]

1.5. Deep Case model redefined

The Lexicalist-Deep Case hypothesis, as outlined
above, will serve as framework for my description of
German nominalization and complementation. However,
several modifications--suggested in Jane Robinson's
Case, Category and Configuration (1970)--have been
incorporated. Chomsky (1965:66-68) illustrates that
relational (functional) notions should not be in the
tree, but that they are redundant, since they can be
configurationally defined. It is precisely at this
point where Fillmore's proposal fails, since he
obviously mixes categorial and functional notions in
a way that Chomsky wanted to avoid. But as Robinson
points out: (1) Chomsky's attempt to define relations
configurationally is only partly successful, and
(2) he is not able to avoid mixing these notions
either. I shall briefly restate the argument.

As Robinson notices, the 'procedure for defining
relationships by configuration will not work for any
construction that contains more than one occurrence

of the same category among its immediate constituents'
(66). In Chomsky (1967), however, the following
rules are proposed:

- (i)   NP ———⟶ N Comp
- (ii)   VP ———⟶ V Comp
- (iii)   AP ———⟶ A Comp
- (iv) Comp ———⟶ NP, NP S, Prep-P, Prep-P Prep-P, etc.

Commenting on these rules, Robinson writes:

> 'COMP is a suspicious category; it looks more
> like a cover term for "whatever else occurs in
> the XP besides the X", so that the division of
> the phrase is less like an immediate constituent
> analysis than like a dependency analysis,
> distinguishing between the HEAD or GOVERNOR
> and its dependents (i.e. complements). This
> is borne out by the fact that the strings
> replacing Comp may not resemble each other at all,
> having no categories in common. Moreover, one
> rewriting of Comp contains two occurrences of the
> same category, Prep-P - i.e. two prepositional
> phrases. It is doubtful that these phrases are
> more meaningfully and individually related to
> each other and to Comp than they are to the N,
> V, or A of the larger phrase' (67-68).

The important thing is that it is not possible to define
the relationship (Prep-P, $\overline{X}$) unambiguously without
labeling the various occurrences of the same category
in some way; this is similar to Fillmore's problem.
With regard to the second point, let us recall that
Chomsky handles the restrictions between Verbs and
Prepositional Phrases by rewriting Prep-phrases as:

$$\text{Prep-Phrase} \longrightarrow \begin{Bmatrix} \text{Direction} \\ \text{Duration} \\ \text{Place} \\ \text{Frequency} \\ \text{etc.} \end{Bmatrix} \qquad (1965{:}102).$$

He then uses the terms so introduced as strict
subcategorization features for the Verb preceding the
Prep-phrase. 'But', Robinson states,

> 'terms like these are not categorial terms any
> more than Locative, Dative, etc. are; and to
> use them in this fashion is simply to turn
> Fillmore's problem on its head. That is,
> Fillmore introduces case terms and rewrites
> them as categories; Chomsky introduces
> categorial terms and re-writes them as something
> suspiciously like case terms. Both wind up with
> preposition plus noun phrase eventually' (71).

Robinson proposes to incorporate Chomsky's distinction

between the <u>Head</u> or <u>Governor</u> and its dependents
(i.e., complements) into Fillmore's deep case model.[8]
The general relationship <u>head</u> <u>of</u> <u>a</u> <u>phrase-complement</u>
is well defined by the categorial component of the
base. Since the categorial component offers no way
to differentiate among the complements, however, she
proposes that 'the lexical component appears to be the
logical place for incorporating case relationships
as primitives' (70).

   As Chomsky (1965:73-74) points out, configurations
allow one also to define a relation between Subject
and Object, which he quite correctly calls an 'irrelevant
pseudorelation'. In order to remedy this defect, he
introduces the notion of selectional restrictions.

   The need to define selectional restrictions in
addition to strict subcategorization is a consequence
of Chomsky's decision to expand the Subject NP directly
under S, so that it is not in an immediate constituent
relation with the Verb and the Object NP's. In
Fillmore's case proposal, on the other hand, all NP's
start out as complements of the Verb and thus there
is no need to ever define selectional restrictions,
since no NP in deep structure occurs outside of the
constituent that immediately dominates V. Thus, for
Fillmore strict subcategorization and selectional

restrictions operate in the same domain.

In order to avoid the defects of Chomsky's and Fillmore's proposals but retain the information that is given by Fillmore's case frames, Robinson suggests simply redefining the cases in the frame 'as positively specified INHERENT FEATURES of the HEADS of the complement constituents, the Ks-in English, the prepositions' (71). This proposal is plausible, since the case features are not inherent features of the Nouns, but rather of Prepositions. Consider, e.g., the sentences:

(16) Mary frightens John.

(17) Sincerity frightens John.

(18) John is frightened by sincerity.

(19) John frightens Mary.

Mary and sincerity are not inherently agentive. The inherent feature that is relevant for grammaticality is the feature [+/-Animate]. Instead of Fillmore's rule

$$N \longrightarrow [+\text{ Animate}] \quad / \quad A, D \; [X \; \underline{\hspace{2cm}} \; Y]$$

Robinson proposes a syntactic redundancy rule of the form

$$N \longrightarrow [+\text{ Animate}] \quad / \quad \begin{Bmatrix} [+\text{ A}] \\ [+\text{ D}] \end{Bmatrix} \underline{\hspace{2cm}}$$

(Robinson 1970:26)

where A and D are not categories as in Fillmore's
proposal but inherent features of the governing
Preposition, which is here regarded as the head of
the complement NP. The following quote from Robinson
summarizes her position:

'The general picture of case and categorial
relations for the constituent P that emerges
from this proposal to interpret cases as
selectional features is one in which the
lexical head of P, the V, has a number of
complements, all of them phrases made up of
a preposition and a noun phrase. The
prepositions are the heads of these phrases.
I use Fillmore's symbol K to denote the
category of prepositions in English and add
the symbol KP to denote prepositional phrases
with the implication that these are case-marked
phrases. Selectional ties exist between the V
and the prepositional heads in its complement.
These are expressed by case features which are
inherent to the category K, and case frame
features restricting the selection of V in
terms of the case features of the prepositions.
Selectional ties also exist between a preposition

and the head of its complement, the N of the NP.
These are expressed by context-sensitive lexical
rules which specify the features for the complex
symbols dominated by Ns which follow Ks with
certain inherent features' (73).

The following diagram, adopted from Robinson (74),
illustrates the structural relationships:

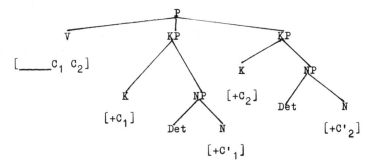

Fig (3): Robinson's dependency structure tree

Robinson explains her notation as follows:

'C_i denotes a CASE FEATURE, [_____ C_i C_j] denotes
a CASE FRAME FEATURE, and C'_i is a CASE-RELATED
FEATURE (like Animate) required of the N when
preceded by C_i in the same KP. In this scheme,
the prepositional category K is selectionally
dominant. The selection of the other
categories is adjusted to the inherent features

of the prepositions by means of the case
frame and case-related features' (74).

The case features of the K's mediate, then, between
the selectional features of the Verb (and Adjective)
and the case-related features of the V and the N,
so that 'the case system is involved with the
relationships holding between all the major parts of
speech, the full lexical stems, and not just with
those involving nouns in complements' (Robinson 1970:77).
This view well coincides with Chomsky's lexicalist
position, where a dependency analysis of the type
<u>head</u> <u>plus</u> <u>complement</u> is advocated.

In order to include Noun complementation in this
schema, i.e., the fact that all three major parts of
speech can occur as lexical heads, Robinson suggests
that the base rules of the grammar are of two forms:

(a) KP ——— K + LP
(b) LP ——— L + KP

(where KP = case-marked phrase with K as its head and
LP = lexical phrase, with L = N, V, or Adj as its head).

1.6. <u>Interpretative</u> <u>vs</u> <u>Generative</u> <u>Semantics</u>

To give a detailed account of the controversy that has
recently divided the Generative camp would lead us
too far afield. However, a few words are necessary
since the conception of the base component depends
upon my stand with regard to the issues concerned.
It has become obvious during the last years that the
Katz-Postal hypothesis, which states that all semantic
information is given in the deep structure of a
sentence, can no longer be maintained in the form
in which it has been proposed.

In order to cope with this problem McCawley,
Lakoff, and others have set out to show that the base
generates semantic structures instead of syntactic
ones, which are then interpreted by the semantic
component. This group has attempted to prove that
there cannot be one distinct level of deep structure
where lexical insertion takes place. One of the main
problems which Generative Semantics will have to cope
with is how to delimit a finite set of semantic
primitives--whether universal or not--which Chomsky's
syntactic base provides naturally.

A second problem for the Generative Semanticists
is how to convert the semantic structures

generated--which for Lakoff e.g., consist of the
semantic representation (SR) and a conjunction of
presuppositions--into a form that can become input
to the syntactic transformations.

The other group referred to as Interpretivists
(including Chomsky, Jackendoff, and others) have coped
with the problem by maintaining the form of the
syntactic component. Instead they have modified
the semantic component, allowing for some semantic
information to be added after the deep structure
level (see, for example, Jackendoff (1972)). It is
this second position which is implicit in the model
of syntactic description which I have chosen.

2. BASE COMPONENT FOR GERMAN

2.1. <u>Preliminary</u> <u>assumptions</u>

In this section I shall outline the form of the base component for German, using the Deep Case model as redefined in section (1.5). I shall assume that the base component consists of a set of context-free phrase structure rules which derive strings of terminal symbols to which lexical items are attached. The resulting structures are interpreted as deep structures of sentences and are then mapped into surface structures by the transformational rules. In spite of recent criticism of the deep structure level,[1] Chomsky (1970) has shown that no arguments have so far been presented that would invalidate such a level. I, therefore, follow Chomsky in assuming a well-defined level of deep structure where the selectional restrictions can be expressed and where lexical insertion takes place.

A derivation is then a set of P-markers $(P_1 \ldots P_i \ldots P_n)$ such that for each P_j, where $1 \leqslant j \leqslant i$, the transformation that converts $P_{j-1} \Longrightarrow P_j$ is a lexical transformation and for each P_j, where $i \leqslant j \leqslant n$, the transformation that converts $P_j \Longrightarrow P_{j+1}$ is a non-lexical transformation. In other words only non-lexical transformations apply after the deep structure level. It will probably be necessary to have a second lexical look-up particularly for function words (e.g., all the Locative Prepositions).

The KP's (case-marked phrases) must be understood as a bounded finite set, although I shall not attempt to delimit the number of case categories here. At this point in case research it would be premature to state how many case categories are needed as primitives; it may well turn out that some of the categories used will later be modified or abolished altogether. The case categories will be defined in the metatheory so that no special definitions need be given in the grammar of a particular language. If not all cases are realized in a particular language, this must be stated as peculiar to this language or the metatheory must be reformed.

The various case categories are introduced into the grammar as features under the K-nodes (although

we may at times for simplicity of expression just
refer to the cases themselves.) I shall assume that
there exists a basic order among the K-nodes of each
language, which may differ from language to language.
In the metatheory cases may simply be an unordered
set of semantic primitives which, however, are
realized in a certain order for each individual
language, depending on the total structure of that
language. If this is true, order would be imposed
upon the case categories by the syntactic component
of the particular language. It will, therefore,
be necessary to provide syntactic justification for
the order chosen. Wherever this is possible, it will
be done here.

Transformations will be assumed to be
meaning-preserving. Although problems with this
principle have been pointed out repeatedly, most
linguists are not ready to give up the principle that
transformations do not change meaning. It must,
however, be understood as a working hypothesis
only that can be abolished if it turns out to be
untenable and not as an established part of the
metatheory, as has frequently been done. If this
principle does not hold for certain aspects, such
as quantifiers and focus, e.g., they can then be

excluded from it. See,e.g., Jackendoff's (1972)
proposal. This, however, in no way implies that the
principle itself has to be abandoned.

2.2. Base rules

The following base rules are needed for German:

$$\text{Rule 1:} \qquad S \longrightarrow \# \begin{Bmatrix} \text{Op} & \text{Prop} & \text{Mod} \\ \text{Conj} & \text{S} & \text{S} & \text{(S)}^* \end{Bmatrix} \# \qquad \begin{matrix} \text{(a)} \\ \text{(b)} \end{matrix}$$

$$\text{Rule 2:} \qquad \text{Op} \longrightarrow \text{(Quant)} \quad \text{(Neg)} \begin{Bmatrix} \text{Declarative} \\ \text{Question} \\ \text{Imperative} \end{Bmatrix}$$

$$\text{Rule 3:} \qquad \text{Mod} \longrightarrow \text{(Perf)} \quad \text{(Aux)} \begin{Bmatrix} \text{Tns} \\ \text{Aspect} \end{Bmatrix}$$

$$\text{Rule 4:} \qquad \text{Prop} \longrightarrow \text{(KP)} \quad \text{(KP)} \quad \text{(KP)} \ldots \text{Vb}$$

$$\text{Rule 5:} \qquad \text{KP} \longrightarrow \text{K} \quad \text{LP}$$

$$\text{Rule 6:} \qquad \text{LP} \longrightarrow \begin{Bmatrix} \text{(L)} + \text{S} \\ \text{D} + \text{N} \end{Bmatrix}$$

2.2.1. Explanation of base rules

Rule 1 has been adopted from the UESP grammar
(1968). The junctures (#) are needed for stating
certain transformations and may also be utilized to
block P-markers which are not well-formed, i.e., any
surface tree in which a juncture symbol appears

internally will be thrown out. Rule 1(a) differs
from the corresponding rule in the UESP grammar in
that the modality appears at the very end. This is
due to my assumption--in agreement with Bach (1962),
Bierwisch (1963), and Bechert, Clément, Thümmel and
Wagner (1970)--that German is an SOV language, i.e.,
the order of the Verb and Modality elements as it
appears in the subordinate clause is the basic pattern
for German. I will justify this decision in conjunction
with the Modality expansion below.[2]

Rule 1(b) contains an iteration symbol (*); this
allows us to generate an indefinite number of conjoined
sentences. The Conjunction is then spread to the
following S's by transformation. Mod (Modality) and
Prop (Proposition) are used in the sense of Fillmore
(1968). The symbol Op (Operator) has been adopted
from P. Seuren (1969). In general we are not concerned
here with the problems of quantification and negation.

Rule 3 states that either Aspect or Tense may
be chosen and that the one excludes the other. I
will assume here that Nominals in German select only
Aspect and Verbs only a Tense element. This will
suffice for the treatment of Nominals, provided that
we can build into rule 3 a constraint which would
guarantee this choice. It may, however, require

modification if the entire verbal system is to be
included in the description. There is some indication
that many verbal prefixes change the Aspect of the
underlying Verb. Consider, for example, <u>kommen</u>, which
has a Durative Aspect and <u>ankommen</u> which can be
interpreted as having an Aorist Aspect. It appears
that some prefixes modify the aspectual meaning of
the Verb. If this fact can be stated in the form of
a number of general rules, we should perhaps allow
Verbs to choose both an Aspect and Tense feature.
The Aspect could then be realized on the surface as
a particular prefix to the Verb itself.

     However, we shall assume here that every Verb
in German is marked with an inherent Aspect feature.
For example, <u>aufstehen</u> always has the Aorist Aspect,
no matter in what Tense or form it appears. <u>Laufen</u>,
on the other hand, is always marked as Durative.
Since many prefixes change not only the Aspect, but
also the basic meaning of the Verb form itself, the
forms with and without a certain prefix must be
treated as different lexical items. Although the
lexical item <u>schlagen</u> is clearly contained in
<u>vorschlagen</u>, it would be difficult to derive the one
from the other, or even more so, to derive all Verbs
with the prefix <u>vor</u> from Verbs without such a prefix.

Such regularities as can be stated in form of
general rules may simply be regarded as lexical rules
that assign a particular Aspect feature to the Verbs
in question before they are introduced into the tree.
This procedure seems justified since Verb forms
consisting of prefix + Verb stem (e.g., an + kommen)
act as a unit and always maintain a particular Aspect,
no matter what its surface realization may be. Thus,
only a Tense feature need be chosen by a Verb in the
deep structure.

For nominalizations, on the other hand, let us
add a constraint to rule 3 stating that only an
Aspect feature but no Tense element is selected.
This hypothetical proposal will be investigated in
chapter 4. If it turns out to be true, the Tense
element can simply be considered as not specified
whenever the nominalized form is in the tree. Our
discussion will be limited to two types of
nominalizations; those forms that nominalize by means
of an ung-suffix and the infinitival Nominals. The
first group of Nominals in ung generally takes on
a Perfective Aspect, the infinitival Nominals, however,
are Duratives, as may be seen from the strings (1) and
(2):

(1)   Die Zerstörung der Stadt ...

(2)   Das Zerstören der Stadt ...

If this treatment should turn out to be correct,
it would mean that the speaker of German, when
deciding between a verbal or nominalized rendering
of a certain underlying structure, is also faced with
the choice between Aspect or Tense. If he chooses
to express a certain Aspect, like the Perfective, he
will select the nominalized form Zerstörung rather
than a finite form of the Verb zerstören. If he wants
to emphasize the Durative Aspect of the particular
Verb he will choose the infinitival das Zerstören.

LP of rule 5 and 6 is a coversymbol for NP,
VP, and AdjP, depending on which one of these three
major parts of speech appears as the lexical head
of the dependent clause. It may, therefore, simply
be realized as D + N. I shall in general use NP
instead of LP, unless it dominates a nominalized
structure with either N, V or Adj as its head.

It will be assumed here that Adjectives and Verbs
form two separate lexical categories in the deep
structure. I shall not attempt to justify this
choice, since this would go beyond the scope of this
study. However, we shall return to this question

again in later chapters whenever it becomes relevant
to the description of complementation and nominalization.
If it should turn out that Verbs and Adjectives form
a natural class with regard to these processes, we
may want to modify our stand on this point.

The expansion LP ——→ (L) + S makes provision
for the embedding of sentences. The introduction of
an optional lexical head in this expansion will be
justified in a later chapter.

The rules which have been given so far are not
sufficient for nominalizations of the form (3):

(3)   Der General verlangt die Zerstörung der
      Stadt durch die Truppen.

In order to include this nominalized structure in our
description the recursive rule 7 is necessary:

Rule 7: LP ——→ (L)   (KP ... KP)   Mod.

The Modality node is required if the choice of Aspect
is associated with the nominalized alternative.

The deep structure of sentence (3) may then be
represented as in (T3):

(T3)

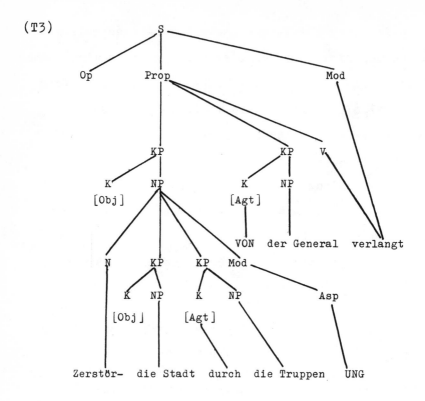

Rule 6 and 7, however, do not give us the simplest possible description. These rules can be conflated into rule 8:

$$\text{Rule 8:} \quad \text{LP} \longrightarrow \left\{ (\text{LP}) \left\{ \begin{array}{l} \text{S} \\ (\text{KP} \ldots \text{KP}) \text{ Mod} \\ \text{Det + N} \end{array} \right\} \right\}$$

2.2.2. Verb and Modal elements

In Esau (1971b) I have proposed a set of rules for
the generation of the German Verb constellation.
Central to my Verb + Modality analysis is the
assumption that the finite Verb occurs sentence-finally
in the underlying structure. Since there are
linguists--notably Ross--who assert that the underlying
sentence structure for German is SVO (Subject Verb
Object) rather than SOV (Subject Object Verb), as I
have suggested, I must briefly review the arguments
which I presented there in support of an SOV analysis.

2.2.2.1. Arguments for and against SOV order in German

The first transformationalist to present arguments
for SOV order in German is Bach (1962). His proposal
is based primarily on formal considerations. Bach
shows that one transformation suffices to relate the
three surface order patterns, due to the different
surface positions of the Verb, if the finite Verb
is generated in sentence final position.

Bierwisch (1963) has presented a number of
syntactic reasons in support of Bach's proposal.
Since I have discussed Bierwisch's evidence in great

detail in Esau (1971b) a mere listing of the arguments
will suffice here:

1. The order for the generation of the verbal
phrase--including the main Verb, Modals and
Auxiliaries--is best stated if all verbal elements
occur sentence-finally, since only there one
continuous sequence of verbal elements exist.

2. The placement of both negative and affirmative
particles must be stated with reference to the Verb.
Only verb-final position permits a unified treatment
for both dependent and independent clauses.

3. The position of separable prefixes points
to a verb-final analysis. If finite Verbs, including
Verbs with separable prefixes, were generated in
second position, the transformation which moves
the finite Verb would have to be formulated so that
it applies to the prefix alone in main clauses but
to prefix + Verb stem in subordinate clauses. For
example, let us assume that sentence (4)

(4) Wir ab + fahren heute abend.

is the underlying structure for both the independent
clause (5) and the dependent clause in (6):

(5) Wir fahren heute abend ab.

(6) Er glaubt, dass wir heute abend abfahren.

In order to derive (5) the transformation must apply
only to the prefix <u>ab</u>, but to derive (6) the entire
Verb <u>ab + fahren</u> is moved. This problem, on the other
hand, is nonexistent if base structures are generated
in which the verbal elements occur sentence-finally.

4. Verbal constructions such as

(7) jemandem etwas zum Geburtstag schenken

are always quoted with dependent clause word order.

5. The same order is obligatory in infinitival
constructions as:

(8) der Versuch, im Haus einen neuen Leiter
zu finden (Bierwisch 1963:35).

6. Bierwisch's verb-proximity principle, which
states that the closer a sentence element is related
to the Verb the shorter will be the distance between
them, is evidence for an underlying SOV structure.
This principle does not hold, unless the Verb is
generated at the end of the clause.

To Bach's and Bierwisch's arguments I have added
a few others (Esau 1971b):

7. Certain impersonal imperatives reflect the
same dependent clause order, for example:

(9) Bitte die Fenster zumachen!

8. The verb-final analysis permits us to explain
why directional and place complements and the associated
Verb can be topicalized together.

9. Within the framework of a Case model an
underlying SVO pattern would also be theoretically
unsound. Given the Case model a sequential order
Verb + Modal can only be generated if the Modality
follows the case phrases, i.e., if it represents the
final element of the string. If the Modality were
generated in front of Prop, i.e., our base rule
(1a) were of the form:

S ⎯⎯⎯⟶ Op   Mod   Prop

the ordering transformations would be much more complex.
In addition a tense jumping rule would have to apply
whenever a Modal or Auxiliary Verb is present in the
string.

10. A number of typological considerations concerning
the positions of Adjectives, relative clause modifiers
and postpositions in SOV languages--which were first
observed and stated by Greenberg (1963)--also support
the assumption that German has an underlying SOV
pattern from which the other surface order patterns
are derived transformationally.

Ross' (1970) evidence in support of an underlying SVO order is confined to his particular analysis of gapping. Gapping--it should be pointed out--represents the only evidence on which Ross' SVO hypothesis rests.[3] In Esau (1971b) I have briefly discussed Maling's (1971) reanalysis of Ross' gapping paper. Maling, I believe, has sufficiently demonstrated that Ross' account of gapping is incorrect. Moreover, it is quite clear that Ross was very selective in the choice of the handful of examples he produces.

In fact gapping in German is quite a complex matter. I have noticed that the native speaker's intuition about which gappings are permissible and which are not is extremely weak. Particularly two factors complicate the gapping processes in German. If the sentence contains a number of syntactically parallel constructions, there may also be a number of ways in which gapping can take place, as in the following examples:

(10a) Er weiss, dass ich immer Pfirsiche bestelle, Peter Kaffe und Hans Kartoffelsalat.

(10b) Er weiss, dass ich immer Pfirsiche, Peter Kaffee und Hans Kartoffelsalat bestellen.

(10c)   Er weiss, dass ich immer Pfirsiche bestelle,
        Peter Kaffee bestellt und Hans Kartoffelsalat.

(10d)   Er weiss, dass ich immer Pfirsiche bestelle,
        Peter Kaffee bestellt und Hans Kartoffelsalat
        bestellt.

(10e)   Er weiss, dass ich immer Pfirsiche bestelle,
        Peter Kaffee und Hans Kartoffelsalat
        bestellt.

It is apparent that the person and number agreement is
important when we try to interpret what has been gapped
and how. It is also clear that there is often more
than one possibility open to the speaker.

A second problem, and the one that is of particular
interest, is the position of the separable prefix in
German. This issue Ross also managed to avoid by
choosing an example of a subordinate clause, where
the prefix does not matter anyway. The following
sentences illustrate that the facts are much more
complicated than Ross would have us believe:

(11)   Ich ziehe mich an und mein Freund aus.

(12)   Ich ziehe mich an und meinen Freund aus.

(13)   Ich ziehe mich an und mein Freund zieht sich au

(14)   Sie ziehen aus und unser Nachbar ein.

(15)   Wir nehmen die Helga und ihr den Franz mit.

(16) Ich war mir meiner Schuld und er sich seiner
Pflicht bewusst.

(17) Martha ist ins Kino und Lotte in die Oper
gegangen.

(18) Ich kenne sie, du ihn, und er kennt alle beide.

While I do not intend to give a description of
gapping here, the examples cited indicate that evidence
from gapping can hardly be considered as sole
justification for determining the position of the Verb
in German. In fact, if one accepts Maling's analysis
gapping, too, supports an underlying SOV order.

Seeing then that all the evidence presented
points toward an underlying SOV pattern for German,
I will assume that the rules which expand Modality
(see base rule 3 above) must be formulated so that
all strings are generated with dependent clause order.
Since the verbal phrase in subordinate clauses forms
a continuous sequence, the order of elements can be
stated without reference to a fictitious Verb + Modal
sequence.

2.2.2.2. <u>Modality</u> <u>expansions</u>

Following I shall briefly restate and exemplify the
Modal expansions as proposed in Esau (1971b). Consider

the following sentences which indicate the range in
complexity of the modality component:

(19a)   Der Wächter wartet auf seine Ablösung.

(19b)   Der Wächter wartete auf seine Ablösung.

(19c)   Der Wächter hat auf seine Ablösung gewartet.

(19d)   Der Wächter hatte auf seine Ablösung gewartet.

(19e)   Der Wächter wird auf seine Ablösung warten.

(19f)   Der Wächter wird auf seine Ablösung gewartet
        haben.

(19g)   Der Wächter muss auf seine Ablösung gewartet
        haben.

(19h)   Der Wächter soll auf seine Ablösung gewartet
        haben müssen.

(19i)   Der Wächter wird auf seine Ablösung gewartet
        haben müssen.

The following rules introduce all the verbal, modal
and tense elements, except for the main Verb--introduced
in base rule 4--which immediately precedes them. These
rules will give us the correct subordinate structures
in each instance, no matter how complex the sentence is:

Rule 3: (i)   Mod $\longrightarrow$ (Perf)   (Aux) $\begin{Bmatrix} \text{Tns} \\ \text{Asp} \end{Bmatrix}$

         (ii)   Aux $\longrightarrow$ (Aux)   M   (Perf)

$$\text{(iii)} \quad \text{Perf} \longrightarrow \text{Af}_p + \begin{Bmatrix} \text{HAB-} \\ \text{SEI-} \end{Bmatrix}$$

$$\text{(iv)} \quad \text{M} \longrightarrow \text{Inf} + \begin{Bmatrix} \text{KÖNN-} \\ \text{MÜSS-} \\ \text{WOLL-} \\ \text{SOLL-} \\ \text{DÜRF-} \\ \text{MÖG-} \end{Bmatrix}$$

$$\text{(v)} \quad \text{Tns} \longrightarrow \begin{Bmatrix} \text{(Fut)} \quad + \quad \text{Fin}_1 \\ \text{Fin}_2 \end{Bmatrix}$$

$$\text{(vi)} \quad \text{Fut} \longrightarrow \begin{Bmatrix} \text{Inf} \quad + \quad \text{WERD-} \\ \emptyset \end{Bmatrix}$$

Af_p = participle marker

Inf = infinitive marker which is
realized on the surface as _en_.

Fin_1 = present tense marker

Fin_2 = past tense marker

As can be seen from rule 3 (ii) and 3 (iii) the introduction
of every verbal element in addition to the main Verb
triggers the introduction of a non-finite marker,
which is then attached to the preceding element.
The finite marker triggered by the main Verb is attached
to the last verbal form in the string. In rule 3 (ii)
I follow Bierwisch (1963), who proposes that the
presence of more than one Modal Verb in a sentence is
to be accounted for by self-embedding. This would

explain why grammaticality in such sentences steadily
decreases as the number of Modals increases. In cases
of repeated embeddings such a deterioration is to be
expected.

I shall assume that Fut + Fin_1 is chosen for
all sentences in which the action or event is
interpreted as belonging to the future. If the
Fut $\longrightarrow \emptyset$ expansion is selected, only the present
tense marker will remain and the surface Verb will
consequently be realized in present tense.

To derive sentence (19a) only Tns occurs under
Modality, so that the deep structure may be rendered
as (20):

(20) Der Wächter auf seine Ablösung WART + Fin_1

The verb-fronting transformation takes the two last
elements in the string (in this case <u>WART + Fin_1</u>)
and moves them to a place after the first NP,
<u>der Wächter</u> to give us sentence (19a).

For sentence (19i) the following derivation
applies (I shall not worry here about lexical insertion
and other irrelevant details, but concern myself solely
with the derivation of the Modal elements):

Rule (i) Der Wächter auf seine Ablösung WART-

$$\text{Perf Aux Tns}$$

   (ii) doesn't apply

  (iii) ... WART Af_p + HAB Aux Tns

   (iv) ... WART Af_p + HAB Inf + Müss Tns

    (v) ... WART Af_p + HAB Inf + Müss Fut Fin_1

   (vi) ... WART Af_p + HAB Inf + Müss Inf

$$+ \text{ WERD }\ \text{Fin}_1$$

If we were aiming for a complete description, lexical
insertion would, of course, have to take place after
rule (vi) has applied to the input string. A general
convention attaches all affixes to the preceding verb
stem. By the time the verb-fronting transformation
applies the string will be of the form:

Der Wächter auf seine Ablösung WART + Af_p

HAB + Inf Müss + Inf WERD + Fin_1

After the verb-fronting transformation the derived
phrase marker will be of the form:

Der Wächter WERD + Fin_1 auf seine Ablösung WART + Af_p

HAB + Inf Müss + Inf

resulting ultimately in the surface string (19i).

3. TRANSFORMATIONAL COMPONENT

3.1. Preliminary Remarks

In the following section I shall briefly sketch
some of the main transformational steps needed to
derive surface structures from the output of the
base component. I have chosen only those transformations
that are immediately relevant to the description of
nominalization and complementation.

If the phrase structure rules of the preceding
chapter are assumed for German, the base component
will yield output strings consisting of a number of
KP's followed by the Verb and the Modality elements.
Base rule 4, which expands Prop into a number of KP's
and Vb, reflects an order that is language-specific.
If it should turn out that such a rule is universal,
it may be preferable to introduce the case categories
as an unordered set in the base and introduce the
language-specific ordering with an early transformation.[1]

In order to permit the simplest description of all
grammatical strings of the language, I shall assume
that the case categories in the base are ordered, until
such a time that it makes sense to talk about something
like a universal base. It should be kept in mind,
however, that the linear order of syntactic case
phrases is language-specific. In other words, it is
an order which the syntax of a particular language
imposes on the universal set of semantic case categories
and which depends primarily on the total structure
of that language.

3.2. Case categories and their order

The first task will be to define a closed set of case
phrases. To account for all the data presented here,
the following deep case categories are needed:

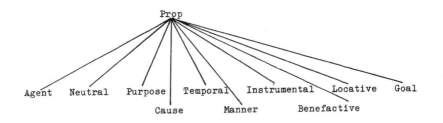

Fig (1): Case categories posited for German

Left to right order in the tree diagram is here assumed
to represent the neutral order of case phrases in a

German utterance. The adopted sequence Agent + Neutral
will be discussed below. For the order among the
remaining case phrases consider the following sentences:

    (1a)   Er hält sich aus dem Grunde jeden Tag so
           lange bei ihm auf.

    (1b) *Er hält sich so lange aus dem Grunde jeden
           Tag bei ihm auf.

    (1c) *Er hält sich so lange bei ihm aus dem Grunde
           jeden Tag auf.

    (2a)   Der Spieler schleudert den Ball aus dem
           Grunde so mit der Hand gegen die Wand.

    (2b) *Der Spieler schleudert den Ball so deshalb
           mit der Hand gegen die Wand.

    (2c) *Der Spieler schleudert den Ball mit der
           Hand so deshalb gegen die Wand.

    (3a)   Der Knabe hat die roten Rosen für die
           Geliebte mit eigener Hand auf der Heide
           gebrochen.

    (3b) ? Der Knabe hat die roten Rosen mit eigener
           Hand für die Geliebte auf der Heide gebrochen.

    (3c) ? Der Knabe hat die roten Rosen auf der Heide
           mit eigener Hand für die Geliebte gebrochen.

I will assume for now that the most neutral surface
case order reflects the order of deep cases as well,

since otherwise the permutation rules would become
more complicated. Sentences (1a), (2a), and (3a) above
would then indicate the following order of case phrases
in German:

> Neutral (Purpose ◊Cause) Temporal, Manner,
> Benefactive, Instrumental, Locative, Goal.

Purpose and Cause do not normally co-occur. In case
both are present Purpose seems to precede Cause as
in (4):

> (4)   Er hat dem Mann deshalb aus Wut gegen den
>   Hosenboden getreten.

and not

> (5)   *Er hat dem Mann aus Wut deshalb gegen den
>   Hosenboden getreten.

3.2.1. Sources of the syntactic category Dative

One important innovation in my description is the absence
of Dative as a universal semantic category. I believe
that the traditional treatment of all types of Datives[2]
indicates sufficiently that Fillmore's definition of
Dative as 'the case of the animate being affected by
the state or action identified by the verb' (1968:24)

does not adequately encompass everything which is supposedly generated under this case node.

German provides ample evidence that Dative represents the result of a merger of several semantic case categories rather than a semantic category proper. We shall not abandon Dative, however, since it appears to be syntactically relevant. It is important to remember here that the case phrases as introduced with base rule 4 represent syntactic nodes in the sense of Robinson (1970) and not semantic deep cases as originally proposed by Fillmore (1968). The syntactic KP's are merely aligned with semantic deep cases by means of the case marker, i.e., the prepositional head of a particular KP. Thus I am claiming that only the semantic categories are universal but not the syntactic KP's with which they align, presumably in some language-specific manner. If the evidence confirms my contention this would indicate that the base does not generate semantic strings, but rather syntactic structures which are in some language-specific way aligned with the universal set of deep case categories. I will show below (i) that a syntactic node Dative must be assumed for an adequate syntactic description of German and (ii) that the syntactic Dative case phrase cannot represent a

universal semantic category. Consider now the following
sentences:

    (6a)   Ich vergüte meinem Freund den Schaden.

    (6b)   Ich vergüte den Schaden für meinen Freund.

    (7a)   Der Wirt gibt dem Reisenden den Zimmerschlüssel

    (7b)   *Der Wirt gibt den Zimmerschlüssel für den

            Reisenden.

    (8a)   Der Gelehrte kaufte seiner Frau den Roman.

    (8b)   Der Gelehrte kaufte den Roman für seine Frau.

    (9a)   Der Junge zerbrach ihr die Vase.

    (9b)   Der Junge zerbrach die Vase für sie.

Let us see if the two semantic categories Goal and
Benefactive posited above suffice to cover the various
interpretations of all surface Datives in the preceding
examples. Sentence (6a) has only one interpretation:

    (10a)   I am making amends to my friend for the
             damage.

where to indicates that the NP my friend functions as
the Goal of the action. The Benefactive interpretations:

    (10b)   *I am making amends for the damage for the
             sake of my friend.

and (10c)   *I am making amends for the damage in his
             stead.

are not possible. Sentence (6b) on the other hand does
not permit a Goal interpretation but may be paraphrased
as:

(10c) I am making amends for. the damage in his
stead.

Sentence (7a) has only a Goal interpretation. In
addition, we infer from the ungrammaticality of (7b)
that geben does not permit the Benefactive reading
for the surface Dative dem Reisenden. Sentence (8a)
has again two readings. The first reading interprets
the surface Dative seiner Frau as the Goal of the
action. The second reading may be paraphrased as:

(12a) The scholar bought the novel for the sake
of his wife.

Here the novel is intended for her, but she need not be
present as goal of the action to receive it, as would
be required with Verbs like geben, schenken, etc.
But notice that the Benefactive reading

(12b) The scholar bought the novel in her stead

is not possible. (12b), however, is one of the two
readings of (8b), the second reading being (12a).
Sentence (9a) does not permit a Goal interpretation
at all, but it may be paraphrased with for her sake.

The reading in which <u>her</u> is interpreted as <u>in her stead</u>
is not permissible. Sentence (9a), however, has a
second reading in which the surface Dative <u>ihr</u> is
derived from an underlying possessive as in (13):

(13)   Der Junge zerbrach die Vase

[sie hat eine Vase]

This last source of the surface Dative will be ignored
here. Sentence (9b) may be paraphrased either as
<u>for her sake</u> or <u>in her stead</u> but a Goal reading is
not possible.

It appears then that Benefactive has two readings:
the weak Benefactive <u>for the sake of</u> and the strong
Benefactive <u>instead of</u>. I shall refer to these two
readings from now on as Ben I and Ben II respectively.
Only the Ben I reading is possible for strings
containing a surface Dative. Sentences with <u>für + NP</u>
permit both a Ben I and a Ben II interpretation. The
Goal interpretation is never possible for the sequence
<u>für + NP</u>. In addition we have seen that surface
Datives can be ambiguous between Goal and Ben I as,
e.g., sentence (8a). But some surface Datives such
as (9a) permit only the Ben I reading, others like
(6a) and (7a) have only a Goal reading. Our results
may be sketched as Fig (2):

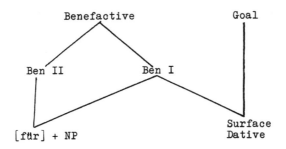

Fig (2): Sources of surface Datives in German

The above graph is, however, incomplete since it is
not true that all Goal phrases are realized as surface
Datives as the graph would suggest. Consider, e.g.,
the following sentences:

(14a) Er hat es mir gesagt.

(14b) Er hat es zu mir gesagt.

(15a) Das Mädchen bringt ihrem Lehrer den Apfel.

(15b) Das Mädchen bringt den Apfel zu ihrem Lehrer.

(16a) Kafka ging selten zu seinem Vater.

(16b) *Kafka ging selten seinem Vater.

The Goal interpretation in sentences (14a) and (15a)
is not as emphatic as in (14b) and (15b). With Verbs
of motion only the zu + NP sequence is permitted
indicating that the strong Goal interpretation is
obligatory here. We find then the same surface
Dative/Prep + NP alternation for Goal phrases as
could be observed for Benefactive phrases, so that

Fig (2) must be modified to Fig (3):

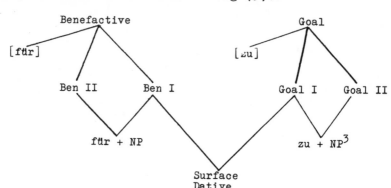

Fig (3): Revised schema indicating the sources
of surface Datives

The traditional category Dative represents thus
a merger of Ben I and Goal I. It is not a semantic
deep category at all but rather a syntactic category
which German has aligned in this language-specific
way with the semantic categories Ben and Goal.

3.2.2.   Evidence for a deep syntactic category Dative

So far no evidence has been given to demonstrate that
a distinct syntactic node Dative is absolutely needed.
Both Benefactives could,e.g., just as well be treated
under one node Ben, perhaps with two sub-nodes. I
will show below, however, that it is necessary to read
off the domain of the VP. Since only Ben I can appear
as surface Dative within the VP but not Ben II, it

would be undesirable to derive both Ben I and Ben II
under one syntactic node.

Chomsky (1965) pointed out that some Time and
Place phrases are closer related to the Verb of the
sentence than others. He proposed to capture this
distinction by introducing Place and Time Adverbials
both under PredP and under VP. The same distinction
must in some way be made in German.

Since the Subject and Object functions are not
defined in the underlying structure of a case grammar,
it is not possible to read off the VP at the deepest
level. I shall tentatively propose that VP is a
derived syntactic grouping definable in terms of the
phrase marker which represents the output of the
subject placement transformation. Since subject
placement appears to be an early rule of the grammar
and the syntactic grouping VP is relevant primarily
for the structural description (SD) of the permutation
and VP-proform-substitution rules, this proposal seems
plausible. Consider the following sentences:

(17a) Der Dieb hat das Geld im Park unter der
       Bank versteckt.
(17b) *Im Park hat der Dieb das Geld unter der
       Bank versteckt.[4]

(17c) *Unter der Bank hat der Dieb das Geld im
Park versteckt.

(17d) Im Park unter der Bank hat der Dieb das
Geld versteckt.

(18a) Die Autos stehen in Deutschland auf den
Dächern.

(18b) In Deutschland stehen die Autos auf den
Dächern.

(18c) *Auf den Dächern stehen die Autos in
Deutschland.

(18d) *In Deutschland auf den Dächern stehen
die Autos.

It has been noted above that only one sentence element
can normally precede the finite Verb in a sentence.
The grammaticality of (17d) demonstrates that im
Park unter der Bank represents one Locative phrase
with two subnodes since they can only prepose together.
The corresponding sentence (18d) is not grammatical,
however, indicating that in Deutschland and auf den
Dächern cannot be considered as one Locative phrase.[5]
Notice also that the two Locative phrases cannot
be used interchangeably, since only in Deutschland
can be preposed to the finite Verb. If we apply a
Locative phrase deletion test we notice further that

deletion of the compound Locative <u>im Park unter der Bank</u>
results in the grammatical string:

    (19)   Der Dieb hat das Geld versteckt.

The corresponding deletion of <u>in Deutschland auf den
Dächern</u>, however, would result in the ungrammatical
string

    (20) *Die Autos stehen

assuming we do not want the contrast reading <u>Die Autos
liegen nicht</u>, <u>sie stehen</u>. A grammatical string results,
however, if the Locative <u>in Deutschland</u> alone is deleted:

    (21)   Die Autos stehen in der Garage.

Thus <u>in Deutschland</u> in (18a) and <u>im Park unter der Bank</u>
in (17a) appear to be Locative phrases of a looser
type than the Locative <u>auf den Dächern</u> in (18a). This
distinction between two types of Locatives is necessary
for other Verbs as well; for example, the deletion of
the Locative phrase <u>in Spanien</u> in

    (22)   Günter kauft ein Haus in Spanien

results in the grammatical string

    (23)   Günter kauft ein Haus.

The deletion of the same Locative phrase in (24)

    (24)   Helga bleibt in Spanien

is not possible, however, since <u>Helga bleibt</u> is
presumably underlyingly <u>Helga bleibt hier</u>.

    If a VP substitution test is applied to the above
sentences, it becomes clear that the deletable Locative
phrases in all instances are not part of the VP but
the non-deletable ones are:

    (25)   Günter kaufte ein Haus in Spanien und ich
            tat dasselbe in England.[6]

    (26)   In Deutschland stehen die Autos auf den
            Dächern, in Amerika tun sie das auch.

but   (27) *Helga bleibt in Spanien und Otto tut
            dasselbe in Frankreich.

    (28) *Auf den Dächern stehen die Autos in Deutschland
            auf der Strasse tun sie das auch.

Thus in order to (i) state the permutation rules and
the VP-substitution transformation correctly and (ii)
explain the recoverability of deleted Locatives such
as <u>hier</u> in <u>Helga bleibt (Loc)</u>, Locative phrases must
be capable of being embedded either under the derived
syntactic grouping VP or outside of it.

3.2.3. <u>Directional</u>, <u>Locative</u>, <u>and</u> <u>Temporal</u> <u>Complements</u>

Following Bierwisch (1963) I will assume that
Directional, my Goal phrase, is the left sister of V,
both of which are dominated by a common node Verbal (Vb).
There is syntactic evidence to indicate that Goal is
closer related to the Verb than all other case phrases.
This fact has also been captured in Bierwisch's
proximity-to-Verb-principle which assumes Directional
or Goal phrases to immediately precede the Verb in
the underlying structure.

It is convenient to consider Directional and Verb
under one noae in order to state the placement of
negative and positive Adverbs such as <u>nicht</u>, <u>nie</u>,
<u>bestimmt</u>, etc. since they immediately precede the
Directional and Verb but cannot be introduced between
them. The complement relationship of the Directional
phrase to the Verb is clearly seen by the fact that
Directionals such as <u>nach Hause</u> in

(29) Wir fahren morgen nach Hause

cannot be deleted without resulting in an ungrammatical
string. The statement of the permutation rules also
requires that Goal phrases are analyzed as complements
of the Verb. Sentence (30)

(30)   Nach Hause gefahren ist er nicht

indicates that the topicalization transformation can
analyze the unit Goal + Verb as one sentence element,
which is possible only if the underlying structure
Fig (4) is assumed:

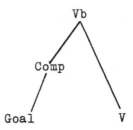

Fig (4):   DS configuration for Goal complements

I will show below that this structure allows us to
express the relatedness between alternating Locative
particles and Prepositions as well.

Locative phrases which are part of the VP function
exactly like Goal phrases.   Thus only sentences (31a)
and (b) are grammatical:

(31a)   Er ist nicht zu Hause geblieben.

(31b)   Er ist bestimmt zu Hause geblieben.

but not

(32a)   *Er ist zu Hause nicht geblieben.

(32b)   *Er ist zu Hause bestimmt geblieben.

Similarly the topicalization rule can prepose units consisting of [Loc + Verb]$_{Vb}$ as in:

(33)   Zu Hause bleiben wollte er nie.

It appears then that Directional complements of the Verb are replaced by Locative complements in cases where the Verb does not permit motion, as in the static Verbs <u>stehen</u>, <u>bleiben</u>, and <u>sein</u>. Syntactic evidence indicates that both the Directional complements and Locative complements with a few static Verbs ought to be treated the same way. We will, therefore, consider Loc and Goal a disjunctively ordered expansion under Comp, expressed by the linked parentheses in Fig (5):

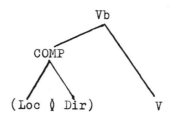

Fig (5):   DS configuration for Locative and
Directional Complements

A few Verbs appear to require a Temporal complement, as, e.g., <u>dauern</u> in:

(34)   Das Spiel dauert nicht lange.

Notice again that (35) and (36) are ungrammatical:

(35) *Das Spiel dauert nicht.

(36) *Das Spiel hat lange nicht gedauert.

But Temp + Verb can be analyzed as a single sentence
element as in:

(37)   Lange gedauert hat das Spiel nicht.

Thus for a few Verbs a third possibility Temp must
be permitted under COMP.

3.2.4.   Bifurcation of case phrases with reference to VP

The tut dasselbe-VP-substitution test shows that
Dative, Neutral--if not subjectivalized--and everything
under Vb are included in the VP after subject placement
has occurred.   All other case phrases are then outside
of the VP.   This proposed bifurcation between sentence
elements within the VP and those without the VP--other
than the Subject--corresponds exactly to Bierwisch's
(1963:49ff.) distinction between the 'aus Adv
abgeleiteten Segmente des Satzes' (50) and other
sentence elements.

Bierwisch has pointed out that the sentence elements
which I have shown to be part of the derived syntactic
grouping VP can only be selected if the Verb is marked
for them. All case phrases which are not part of
the VP so defined can be optionally introduced with
almost all Verbs in the language.[7]

Bierwisch also observed that the case phrases
outside of the VP can 'in beschränktem Masse ausserhalb
des sogenannten Satzrahmens an das Ende des Satzes
gestellt werden' (50). The bifurcation is also
reflected in the surface realization of the case phrases.
The case phrases within the VP except for those under
COMP are normally realized without a preposition
whereas all case phrases outside of VP are prepositionally
marked.

From the evidence presented above we may deduce
that it is necessary to define the syntactic grouping
VP at some point in the derivation, presumably in
terms of the phrase marker (PM) that represents the
output of the subject placement transformation. If
my analysis of Dative as a merger of Ben I and Goal I
is correct, we should expect to find Ben I to be part
of the VP when it merges into the syntactic category
Dative. Whenever Ben is realized as __für + NP__, on
the other hand, it should function with the case

phrases that are not part of the VP.

Let us test this expectation and apply the
VP-substitution test to sentences (8a) and (8b) above:

(38a)   *Der Gelehrte kaufte seiner Frau den Roman
         und ich tat meiner dasselbe.

(38b)   Der Gelehrte kaufte den Roman für seine
        Frau und ich tat dasselbe für meine Frau.

Sentence (38a) is ungrammatical since the minimal
unit which <u>tat dasselbe</u> can replace is the entire VP.
It is, therefore, impossible to single out one element
of the second VP and contrast it with an element of
the first VP while at the same time applying the
<u>tat dasselbe</u> substitution to the second VP of the
string. I.e., given my analysis we would have
predicted that sentence (38a) is ungrammatical. On
the other hand, if the Benefactive NP in the second
part of the conjoint is realized outside of the VP
such a contrast should be possible. This conclusion
is again confirmed by the grammaticality of (38c):

(38c)   Der Gelehrte kaute seiner Frau den Roman
        und ich tat dasselbe für meine.

3.2.5. <u>Goal</u> <u>and</u> <u>Benefactive</u> <u>prepositions</u> <u>in</u> <u>nominalizations</u>

Notice also that the assumption of two sources for
the syntactic category Dative explains an apparent
irregularity in certain nominalizations. If sentences
39-41 (a) are expressed as nominalizations, a Goal
Preposition is obligatorily inserted.

(39a)   Er dankt mir.

(39b)   Sein Dank an mich.

(40a)   Er verspricht mir ...

(40b)   Sein Versprechen an mich ...

(41a)   Karl antwortet ihr.

(41b)   Karls Antwort an sie ...

Other nominalizations require the Benefactive Preposition
<u>für</u>:

(42a)   Er kauft ihr die Möbel.

(42b)   Sein Möbeleinkauf für sie ...

(43a)   Herbert malt ihr ein Bild.

(43b)   Herberts Malen des Bildes für sie ...

The evidence presented thus indicates that the assumption
of a merger of two semantic categories into one syntactic
one--here referred to as Dative--allows us to state
and explain a number of syntactic facts not statable

otherwise.   There will then be surface Datives without
prepositional heads from three different sources as
illustrated in the following diagram:

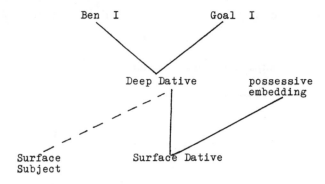

Fig (6): Sources of surface Datives (final version)

3.2.6 Separable prefixes and categorial Prepositions

The parallelism between the frequently alternating
separable prefixes and categorial Prepositions, i.e.,
Prepositions lexically determined by a particular
Verb for an associated case phrase, can also be
expressed by introducing both under COMP.   The
following pairs are grammatical for many speakers:

(44a) Er schreibt an mich.

(44b) Er schreibt mich an.

(45a) Er steht bei mir.

(45b) Er steht mir bei.

(46a) Der Junge malt an die Wand.

(46b) Der Junge malt die Wand an.

Although there is a distinct semantic difference
between most pairs, they are still felt closely related
by the speaker. This should, of course, be expressed
in an adequate syntactic description. The underlying
structures for (44a) and (b) differ only in the form
introduced under COMP. The formative an in (44b)
is simply a Locative Adverb not marked for any
associated KP whereas an in (44a) is a Locative
Preposition marked in the lexicon for the KP which
it relates to the Verb, i.e., $\underset{[+\ \overline{\text{GOAL}}]}{\text{an}}$. The two

formatives an and $\underset{[+\ \overline{\text{GOAL}}]}{\text{an}}$ are related in the lexicon
by functional extension.[8] Thus the syntactic similarity
is expressed by their underlying structural similarity,
whereas the semantic differences are captured by the
fact that the homophonous particles belong to
functionally and semantically distinct classes in
the lexicon. The syntactic consequences will be that
the preposition placement transformation moves an
only if it is marked as belonging to a certain KP.
This transformation places the Preposition in front
of the KP for which it is marked. If an is not
marked for any KP, it is a separable prefix and
remains where it is. Under COMP I am also introducing

the Directional and Place particles which give rise
to doublets like the following:

(47a)   Dahin fahre ich nicht.

(47b)   Da fahre ich nicht hin.

3.3.   Some transformations

Having established a tentative order of the underlying
case phrases we can now turn to a few of the
transformations needed to map the underlying strings
into surface strings of the language.   I assume that
lexical insertion has taken place (as described in
section 2.1), i.e., the output of the last lexical
insertion rule represents the deep structure, which
serves as input to the transformational component.

3.3.1.   Passive transformation

One of the first transformations is the passive rule.
Chomsky (1957) has proposed to derive the passive
sentences transformationally from their active
counterparts.   If this proposal is chosen, which has
also been accepted by Bierwisch (1963) and those
working in his framework, the passive transformation
will look roughly like (48):

(48) X   KP   KP   Y $\dfrac{V}{[+ \text{Pass}]}$ $\overline{\text{Af}}$ Z
      $\overline{1}$ $\overline{2}$ $\overline{3}$ $\overline{4}$ 5

$\Longrightarrow$ 1   3   VON + 2   4 Af_p + WERD   5

Using the base rules introduced earlier the surface
string

(49) Der Präsident ist vom Kabinet schlecht
      beraten worden.

would have the deep structure (50):

(50) Das Kabinet der Präsident schlecht berat-
      Af_p HAB Fin_1.

The passive transformation would yield the following
string:

(51) Der Präsident VON dem Kabinet schlecht berat+
      Af_p WERD + Af_p HAB + Fin_1.

If this procedure is chosen and WERD is introduced
transformationally, we need an adjustment rule that
changes the HAB of (51) into SEI when the passive
Verb WERD is inserted. This complication can be
avoided if the passive WERD is introduced in the phrase
structure rules of the base. We simply have to rewrite
our base rule 3 (i) as:

$$3 \ (\mathrm{i'}) \quad \mathrm{Mod} \longrightarrow (\mathrm{Pass}) \ (\mathrm{Perf}) \ (\mathrm{Aux}) \begin{Bmatrix} \mathrm{Asp} \\ \mathrm{Tns} \end{Bmatrix}$$

In addition we would then need an expansion 3 (vii):

(vii): Pass $\longrightarrow$ $\mathrm{Af_p}$ + WERD

If this second procedure is chosen it will automatically give us the correct perfect auxiliary which depends on the preceding verb form. In case passive is chosen in the base the auxiliary will always be SEI. The presence of $\mathrm{Af_p}$ + $\underset{[+\ \mathrm{Pass}]}{\mathrm{WERD}}$ in the tree triggers the then obligatory passive transformation (52) which can now be stated much simpler:

$$(52) \quad \underset{1}{\mathrm{X}} \ \underset{2}{\mathrm{KP}} \ \underset{3}{\mathrm{KP}} \ \underset{4}{\mathrm{Y}} \ \underset{5}{\mathrm{WERD}} \ \mathrm{Z} \Longrightarrow 1 \ 3 \ 2 \ 4 \ 5$$

The agent case marker VON is preserved whenever the Agent is not subjectivalized, as is normally the case in active sentences.

There exists other evidence which points to the second proposal. The independent generation of active and passive sentences is preferable, since a transformational derivation of the passive from the active sentence seems to give priority to the active alternative. A separate derivation of active and passive from a common underlying structure--depending

on whether or not Pass is selected in the base--not
only avoids the question of priority but it is also
inherent in the case model which does not recognize
a deep Subject at all. Thus the difference between
an active and passive rendering of a certain underlying
string is primarily a difference of the element to
be subjectivalized, i.e., it is primarily a difference
in topicalization.

There is also a semantic consideration which
suggests an independent derivation of active and
passive sentences, as is demonstrated by the following
pair:

(53a) Alle Studenten in diesem Zimmer sprechen
       mindestens zwei Sprachen.
(53b) Mindestens zwei Sprachen werden von allen
       Studenten in diesem Zimmer gesprochen.

Whereas sentence (53a) is unambiguous, sentence (53b)
is ambiguous in that it is not clear whether each
student speaks two languages or in the group of all
students, some speak one language and others another.
Thus (53b) cannot be derived from (53a) unless we are
willing to abandon the principle that transformations
do not change meaning. We shall, therefore, assume
that the passive is derived independently from its

active counterpart and that the passive

transformation--actually a subject placement

transformation--has the form (52).

3.3.1.1. Place of passive within transformationa cycle

The passive transformation is one of the earliest rules

in the grammar. It has to precede the subject placement

transformation; actually they are disjunctively ordered

with regard to one another. If passive is present in

the input phrase marker to the passive transformation

the Object will be fronted. This is necessary since

not all Verbs which can be used actively can also be

used passively. Thus by ordering passive before

active subject placement we are ruling out the more

constrained alternative first and only if passive

has not applied can the more general active alternative

apply. Notice that certain constraints on passive

must be stated before the active subject placement

in any case. Although both the active and passive

(54a) and (b) are possible

    (54a) Es wird hier getanzt.
    (54b) Man tanzt hier.

the passive alternative becomes ungrammatical as soon

as a definite NP is added. The interpretation of <u>es</u>
in sentence (54a) as a reflex of an underlying
indefinite Agent NP is supported by the fact that this
<u>es</u> is only possible with the passive if no other
Agent NP is present. Thus

    (55a) Der Mann tanzt.

is grammatical but

    (55b) *Es wird von dem Mann getanzt.

is not. That the Verb <u>tanzen</u> is not inherently marked
as [- Passive] may be seen from the grammaticality
of (56):

    (56) Der Tango wird von dem Mann langsam getanzt.

Thus if the structural description of the input string
to the passive transformation contains neither an
indefinite nor definite Agent phrase the passive
sentence is disallowed. This constraint must be stated
prior to active subject placement, since in these
cases the active sentence becomes obligatory. Therefore,
it will be simpler if the passive precedes the active
subject placement. Passive must also precede
Equi-NP deletion.[9] Consider the derivation of
sentence

(57)   Hans gestattet Günther, vom Arzt untersucht
       zu werden.

from the deep structure (58):

(58)   VON + Hans Günther NP gestatt + Fin_1
       [VON + der Arzt Günther untersuch + Af_p
                                    WERD + Fin_1].
       [+ Pass]

If Equi-NP deletion were to precede the passive
transformation the structural description for passive
would not be met and could not be generated. Therefore,
the passive has to apply first to give us:

(59)   VON + Hans Günther NP gestatt + Fin_1
       [Günther VON + der Arzt untersuch + Af_p
                                    WERD + Fin_1]
       [+ Pass]

At this point Equi-NP deletion can apply. It deletes
the Subject NP of the embedded S to give:

(60)   Hans Günther $_S$[vom Arzt untersuch + Af_p
                                    WERD + $Fin_1]_S$

       gestatt + Fin_1

After gestatt + Fin_1 is fronted all remaining Fin-markers

are converted into Inf-markers to give us the surface
string (57).

3.3.2. <u>Equi-NP</u> <u>deletion</u>

The Equi-NP deletion transformation requires more
discussion. Deletion transformations are the most
powerful devices in Transformational Grammar; for this
reason it is desirable to constrain deletions as much
as possible without excluding any grammatical strings
from the generated language. I shall assume, therefore,
that the recoverability principle proposed by Katz
and Postal (1964) (although perhaps in a slightly
weaker form) applies to German as well. This principle
implies that anything which is deleted during the
transformational process must in general be recoverable.
It is easy to see why this should be so, remembering
that our goal is to describe the competence of the
ideal speaker-hearer. The hearer must be able to
reconstruct any deleted elements that represent part
of the meaning of the sentence in order to interpret
correctly what he hears.

Although other types of NP deletion must be assumed
for German, for instance indefinite NP deletion or
an optional lexical head noun deletion, I shall be

concerned only with Equi-NP deletion. The main question
is how the speaker-hearer knows which of several
underlying NP's has been deleted. In other words,
what is the principle--if there is a single one--that
permits the hearer to go backwards from the PM which
is the output of the Equi-NP deletion and to decide
unequivocally which NP has been deleted. The problem
may be demonstrated with the following sentences:

(61) Der Mann zwingt seinen Sohn, zur Schule
zu gehen.

(62) Der Junge geht zur Schule, um etwas zu
lernen.

In sentence (61) the deleted NP is coreferential with
the Object of the matrix sentence while in sentence (62)
the deleted NP is coreferential with the Subject of the
matrix.

3.3.2.1. Rosenbaum's principle of minimal distance

Rosenbaum (1967) was the first to state the erasure
principle for English in a systematic way. However,
his principle of node counting is much too ad hoc to
be considered explanatorily adequate. It has now been
largely abandoned for it is not even observationally

adequate as may be seen from the following sentence:

(63) Der Junge hat den Mut, ins Wasser zu springen.

According to Rosenbaum's principle of minimal distance
the deleted NP should be identical to that NP of the
matrix sentence to which it is closest if the intervening
branches are counted. This, however, is hardly true
for sentence (63) no matter how we draw the tree as
may be seen from (T63):

(T63)

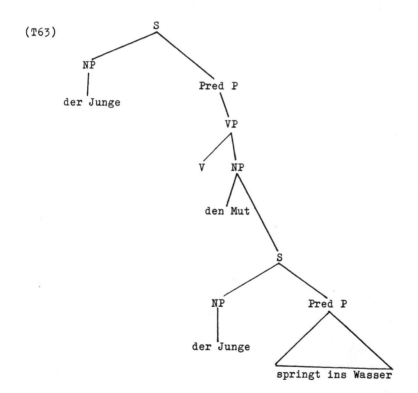

The NP <u>den Mut</u> is closest to the embedded Subject NP;
thus the principle of minimal distance does not permit
us to reconstruct the deleted NP in this case.

3.3.2.2. <u>UESP's</u> <u>erasure</u> <u>principle</u>

In an attempt to fill in this embarrassing gap the
UESP grammar has proposed 'that the erasing NP is
identified by the case node dominating it, and replaced
the principle of minimum distance by the principle
that an identical dative has erasure priority over an
identical agent' (1968:2.559). However, this proposal
does not seem to work for German either. Consider,
e.g., the sentences:

>   (64)   Wir raten Ihnen, die Türe abzuschliessen.
>   (65)   Er täuscht ihr vor, nichts davon zu wissen.

In sentence (64) the deleted NP is coreferential with
the Dative NP of the matrix sentence, in (65), however,
with the Agent NP.

3.3.2.3. <u>Concluding</u> <u>remarks</u>

It appears that the Verb itself determines to some
extent which NP can be deleted. <u>Raten</u> belongs to a
class of Verbs which require that the deleted NP in
their complements be coreferential to the Dative NP

of the matrix sentence. Other Verbs of this class
are: <u>befehlen</u>, <u>empfehlen</u>, <u>erlauben</u>, <u>gestatten</u>,
<u>verbieten</u>, etc. <u>Vortäuschen</u>, on the other hand,
belongs to a class of Verbs which require that the
deleted NP in its complement be coreferential to the
Agent NP of the matrix sentence. To this group
belong further: <u>hoffen</u>, <u>behaupten</u>, <u>versuchen</u>,
<u>vergessen</u>, <u>versprechen</u>, etc.

In some cases the deleted NP is predictable from
known properties of the complements and can be read
up from the surface structure. E.g., in the case of
an <u>um zu</u>-complement the speaker knows that the deleted
NP has to be identical to the surface Subject. It
is doubtful whether a unique principle of erasure
can be determined for all cases of NP deletion.
Therefore, the attempt to establish one for German
may prove futile. The Equi-NP deletion transformation
is roughly of the form (66):

(66) SD: $\quad$ $\underline{X \quad NP_1 \quad Y}$ $\quad$ $\underline{NP_2}$ $\quad$ $\underline{Z}$
$$\qquad\qquad\qquad 1 \qquad\qquad 2 \quad\ 3$$

$\qquad$ SC: $\Longrightarrow$ 1 $\emptyset$ 3

Condition: NP_1 is coreferential with
NP_2 and the S which expands
NP_2 is immediately embedded
under the S which expands
NP_1.

3.3.3.   Verb fronting transformation

The last transformation to be considered in this section
is verb fronting. Remembering that the finite Verb
is generated sentence-finally; verb-second position in
declarative sentences and verb-first position in
questions and imperatives are considered as derived.
As I have discussed the verb-fronting transformation
in Esau (1971b) I shall here briefly restate my earlier
account. The transformation can be formally stated as:

(67) SD: X KP   Y   Z Fin
                 ‾‾‾‾‾   ‾   ‾‾‾‾‾
                  1   2   3

      SC: $\Longrightarrow$ 1 3 2

where Z is either the main verb or the
rightmost item under Mod. X does not
contain a complementizer or relativizer.

This transformation has the effect of moving the finite
Verb (i.e., that verbal or modal element which is

followed immediately by the tense and person marker
(Fin)) into sentence-second position.

The verb-fronting transformation appears to be
a relatively late rule. Notice that it must follow
the optional preposing of dependent clauses, as the
following reordering indicates:

(68) Wir spielen heute Fussball, wenn es nicht
regnet.

(69) Wenn es nicht regnet, spielen wir heute
Fussball.

If verb-fronting occurs after the constituent sentence

$$_{KP}[\ _{S}[\text{ wenn es nicht regnet }]_{S} \ ]_{KP}$$

has been optionally preposed to the matrix sentence,
it will automatically fulfill the condition of KP
in the structural description of the verb-fronting
transformation. This gives the desired finite verb
position in strings where an embedded sentence precedes
the matrix sentence in the surface structure.

Sentences containing an imperative or question
marker also undergo the verb-fronting transformation.
This way it is possible to account for the fact that
interrogation and command can be realized both by

pitch and word order. Thus besides (70) the speaker
can also say (71):

    (70)   Gehen sie morgen ins Kino?

    (71)   Sie gehen morgen ins Kino?

And besides (72) he can also use (73)

    (72)   Gehen Sie jetzt bitte nach Hause!

    (73)   Sie gehen jetzt bitte nach Hause!

where interrogation in sentence (71) and command in
(73) are realized through pitch rather than word order.
The verb-fronting transformation, which is a general
transformation in the grammar, can thus be made
obligatory for all declaratives, imperatives, and
interrogatives. The question and imperative word
order transformation then inverts the Subject and the
finite Verb. This transformation has to optionally
permit both command and question to be realized through
pitch. W-questions can be accounted for by introducing
into the subject-verb inversion transformation a
condition such as:

    (74) $\underset{[\text{Subject}]}{X} \neq$ W-word

3.3.4. Other syntactic rules

Before the assignment of surface cases all case features
have to be copied from the Prepositions--which at
this point still follow the Nouns--into the Nouns
themselves. We can at the same time introduce an
affix segment following each Noun into which eventually
the case endings will be introduced. Thus we need
the following rule in our grammar:

$$(75) \quad \emptyset \longrightarrow \text{Aff}/ \begin{bmatrix} + \text{ NOM} \\ + \text{ stem} \end{bmatrix} \underline{\quad\quad\quad} [\text{prep}].$$

An important block of syntactic rules are the
surface case assignment rules. They represent an
ordered set to be applied obligatorily. I am merely
suggesting a scheme here for setting up these rules.
First, it will be necessary to determine the KP
environment for the Verbs in the language. For
example, geben belongs to a class of Verbs marked
for the following case frame: GEBEN [Agt, Neut, Dat ___].
The first of the case assignment rules will specify
which KP is to be realized in the Subject case. The
case frame for the Verb geben is one of the environments
for the rule:

$$(76) \quad \text{Agt} \longrightarrow \text{Nominative} \left\{ \begin{array}{ccc} \text{Agt,} & \text{Neut,} & \text{Dat} \\ & \cdot & \\ & \cdot & \\ & \cdot & \end{array} \right\}$$

After all the environments for Nominative have been set
up, the various Object environments are listed. These
rules are then applied until each NP has been marked
for a surface case.

The various permutation transformations which
Bierwisch (1963) has discussed in some detail are
applied after the surface cases have been assigned.
They will produce the stylistic variants in word order.
Many other transformations which I have not even
touched on in the present study will have to be
worked out before it is possible to integrate what
has been said here into a total account of the
transformational component.

4. TRANSFORMATIONAL OR LEXICAL DERIVATION OF NOMINALS

In this chapter the derivation of Nominals in German will be treated in terms of the basic question of whether the parallelism between a Nominal and its verbal cognate is to be expressed in the transformational subcomponent of the grammar or whether it can be more adequately handled in the lexicon.

4.1. Selection principle for Nominal-Verb alternative

4.1.1. Aspect and Tense

I have suggested in Chapter 2 that the difference between the nominalized and the verbal structure might depend on whether Aspect or Tense has been chosen. It is appropriate at this point to test this hypothesis in order to see if this is actually what does happen. Let us consider the following pair of strings:

(1) Er versucht, ihn einzuholen.

(2) Sein Versuch, ihn einzuholen ...

If it is assumed that the Aspect/Tense alternative is
built into the base component, as outlined in the
preceding section, sentence (1) and (2) might then
be derived from the deep structures (T1) and (T2),
respectively:

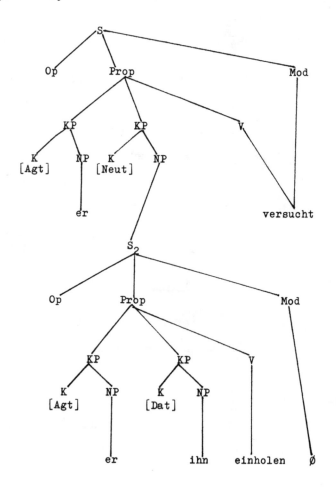

(T2)

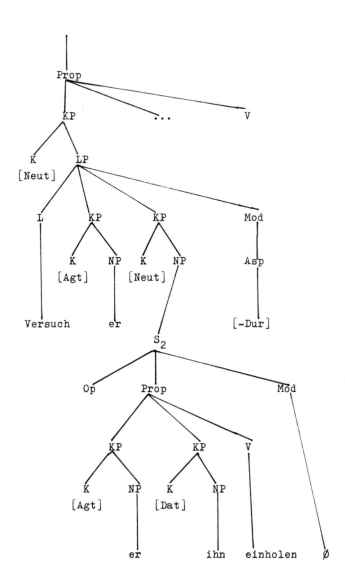

In order to derive string (1) from deep structure
(T1), the Tense element is selected, resulting in the
generation of the verbal form. The Equi-NP deletion
transformation deletes the Agent NP of the embedded
sentence. Another transformation introduces the
zu-complementizer into the embedded sentence. Leaving
aside all irrelevant details, the resulting surface
string will be: Er versucht, ihn einzuholen. To
derive string (2) Aspect is chosen instead of Tense
to ensure the generation of a nominalized structure.
from the deep structure (T2). The Equi-NP deletion
transformation is again applied to remove the Agent
of the embedded clause and introduce the zu-complementizer.
The Agent NP of the matrix sentence is realized as
the possessive sein yielding the surface string
Sein Versuch, ihn einzuholen ...

4.1.2. Topic

It would appear that a syntactic description has been
established which captures the parallelism between
the nominalized structure (2) and the corresponding
string (1) containing its verbal cognate. Moreover,
this description seems to define the mechanism that
determines the choice of the two alternative renderings.

But such a treatment entails several problems. As
long as I select--in accordance with the general
practice of Transformational treatments of
Nominals--nominalizations that are only segments
of sentences, the scheme sketched above seems to work.
However, no speaker of German would normally utter
the fragmentary string <u>Sein Versuch, ihn einzuholen</u> ...
except perhaps as an answer to a question like:
<u>Was hat eigentlich den Polizeiwagen ins Schleudern
gebracht</u>? In this case <u>Sein Versuch, ihn einzuholen</u>
replaces the interrogative <u>was</u> and must, therefore,
be considered the topic of the sentence: <u>Sein
[des Polizisten] Versuch, ihn einzuholen, hat den
Polizeiwagen ins Schleudern gebracht</u>. Now consider
sentences (3) and (4):

(3) Er versucht, ihn einzuholen.

(4) Sein Versuch, ihn einzuholen, geht mir auf
     die Nerven.

Sentence (3) is simply the statement that someone
attempts to catch up with someone else. Nothing is
being said about the action so described. Sentence (4),
however, is not primarily concerned with the description
of the event itself. Instead the whole string (3)
has been topicalized in the nominalized structure (4),

so that the speaker may make a statement about it,
namely, that someone's attempt to catch up to someone
gets on the speaker's nerves. The two strings
<u>Er versucht</u>, <u>ihn einzuholen</u> and <u>Sein Versuch</u>,
<u>ihn einzuholen</u> ... thus have an entirely different
function.

Perhaps the difference is due only to the absence
of the clause <u>... geht mir auf die Nerven</u> in
sentence (3). Consider, therefore, the following
sentences:

   (5a) Es geht mir auf die Nerven, dass er ihn
        einzuholen versucht.
   (5b) Dass er ihn einzuholen versucht, geht mir auf
        die Nerven.

At first it seems as if the <u>dass</u>-complementizer makes
sentences (5a) and (5b) slightly different from
sentence (4) since it emphasizes the notion of
consequence, i.e., S_1 is a consequence of S_2. However,
there is clearly another difference between these
sentences, namely, a difference of topicalization.
This may be illustrated by constructing possible
questions to each of these sentences. Sentence (4)
is a plausible answer to question (6):

   (6) Was geht Ihnen auf die Nerven?

However, sentences (5a) and (5b) are much less natural
as answers to question (6). Now consider question (7):

(7) Was versucht er denn heute, das Ihnen so
auf die Nerven geht?

Sentence (4) is not a possible answer to this question,
since the whole nominalization <u>Sein Versuch, ihn einzuholen</u>
is a topicalization. It would, however, be quite
natural to answer with sentence (5a) <u>Es geht mir auf die</u>
<u>Nerven, dass er ihn einzuholen versucht</u>, or simply
<u>Er will ihn einholen</u>. The reason why sentences (5a) and
(b) are perceived as different from their nominalized
parallel is that only <u>einzuholen</u> is topicalized in
these sentences. It appears then that the choice
between a nominalization and the parallel structure
containing its verbal cognate depends on what the
speaker intends to topicalize rather than whether
he chooses between Aspect and Tense. If the speaker
nominalizes, he topicalizes the entire nominalization.
If he chooses the verbal form, however, he will
generally select one particular element as topic of
the sentence, e.g., <u>einzuholen</u> in sentence (5a).

4.1.3. <u>Tense ambiguity in Nominals</u>

There are other reasons which seem to indicate that

the choice between Aspect and Tense, which we have
hypothetically posited above, is not the correct
analysis. Consider, e.g., the following sentences:

(8)   Wir besprechen heute die Aufwertung der DM.

(9)   Die Aufwertung der DM steht heute zur
      Diskussion.

(10) Seine Verwundung erfahre ich mit Bedauern.

(11) Seine Verwundung nehme ich mit Schmerzen wahr.

(12) Er erlaubt die Entführung des Mädchens nur
      ungern.

(13) Ich bin gegen seine Zerstörung der Stadt.

Sentences (8) and (9) are ambiguous with respect to
Past and Future interpretation of the nominalization
die Aufwertung der DM, although the main Verb is in
the Present Tense and the temporal Adverbial heute
implies that the discussion will take place in the
Future. Sentence (10) can only mean that the Verwundung
is an event of the Past, whereas sentence (11) is
again ambiguous with regard to Tense, Past or Present.
In sentence (12) the nominalized element die Entführung
des Mädchens may either be in progress or it may
still be in the Future. And sentence (13) even
permits Past, Present, and Future interpretation.

    It is clear that it is not the absence of Tense

in the nominalization that we have here but rather
ambiguity of Tense. Furthermore the ambiguity is
unpredictable. In some cases the Verb of the main
sentence imposes certain constraints on the Tense
of the nominalization, e.g., (9) <u>Ich nehme seine
Verwundung wahr</u> could not mean that his injury will
take place in the Future. However, whether the injury
is taking place at the moment of speaking or is already
a thing of the Past is not indicated in the surface
string (9). The only logical conclusion is that
sentence (9) has two deep structures, one containing
the Tense element Present in the structure which
underlies the nominalization <u>Seine Verwundung</u> and
the other with Past as the underlying Tense element.
The Tense element is then deleted if the nominalized
form <u>Seine Verwundung</u> is chosen, whereas it remains
if the speaker uses the verbal structure <u>er ist verwundet</u>
or <u>er war verwundet</u>. In order to prevent the Future
interpretation, the Verb of the main sentence <u>wahrnehmen</u>
must be makred with some feature specifying that an
embedded nominalization may not normally contain a
Future Tense element. A Future interpretation is
e.g., possible in sentence (14):

> (14) Hagen wird Siegfried an der Quelle eine
> Verwundung beibringen.

The introduction of a Tense element in nominalizations
is also needed to account for those cases where time
particles modify a Nominal, as, e.g., in (15):

(15) Ihre heutige Entführung ...

But notice that even with a temporal modifier there
is an ambiguity of Tense as may be seen from
sentence (16) and (17): [1]

(16) Ihre heutige Entführung überraschte uns alle.

(17) Ihre heutige Entführung werde ich verhindern.

From the evidence presented it is clear that an analysis
that makes the selection of nominalized structures
dependent on the choice of Aspect rather than Tense
in the base--which means that the Tense element is
absent in the nominalized deep structure--does not
adequately account for the facts of German. If it is
assumed that the Tense element is present in the deep
structure but that nominalization prevents its
surface realization, it is easy to account for Tense
ambiguity.

4.1.4. Concluding remarks

The question is, then, whether or not an Aspect marker
should be introduced into the tree at all. The

Perfective/Durative distinction between the
ung-nominals and the infinitival Nouns seems to me
to be a useful one and I shall try to justify the use
of Aspect to distinguish between these two groups of
Nominals in the following section. However, it is
clear that an Aspect/Tense alternative should not be
built into the base to trigger either a verbal or a
nominal structure. Whether the speaker says (18) or
(19)

(18)   Der Feind zerstört die Stadt.

(19)   Die Zerstörung der Stadt durch den Feind
       hat uns alle überrascht.

is determined by what he wants to topicalize. One might,
therefore, propose to introduce a topic node into
the deep structure which could be made the basis for
the speaker's choice between the verbal and the
nominal form.

It is generally recognized today that the treatment
of topic belongs to the semantic component and not to
the syntactic component. How a syntactic description
could account for problems of topicalization is,
therefore, difficult to perceive. There are, of course,
syntactic consequences connected with the choice of
topic. Nevertheless, what is to be topicalized is
a semantic phenomenon. It may even be argued that
introducing topic into the syntax means to describe
performance rather than competence. And to introduce
a partly semantic and partly performance phenomenon
into the syntactic component of a competence grammar,
in order to account for the verbal/nominal distinction
is undesirable.

There is a second reason why it would be impossible
to incorporate topic into a syntactic description at
this time. Topic is largely determined by the larger
context or discourse and cannot be defined in terms
of a single sentence as the unit of its operation.

4.2. Incorporation of NOM into base rules

If the above modifications are incorporated, our base
rules of chapter 3 may be rewritten as follows:

Rule 1: $S \longrightarrow \# \begin{Bmatrix} \text{Op} & \text{Prop} & \text{Mod} \\ \text{Conj} & S & S & (S)^* \end{Bmatrix} \#$

Rule 2: $\text{Op} \longrightarrow (\text{Quant}) \ (\text{Neg}) \begin{Bmatrix} \text{Declarative} \\ \text{Question} \\ \text{Imperative} \end{Bmatrix}$

Rule 3: $\text{Prop} \longrightarrow (\text{KP}) \ldots (\text{KP}) \ \text{Vb}$

Rule 4: $\text{KP} \longrightarrow \text{K} \ \text{LP}$

Rule 5: $\text{LP} \longrightarrow \begin{Bmatrix} (\text{L}) & S \\ \text{D} & \text{NOM} \end{Bmatrix}$

Rule 6: $\text{NOM} \longrightarrow \begin{Bmatrix} \text{NOM} & S \\ \text{N} & (\text{KP}) \ldots (\text{KP}) & \text{Mod} \end{Bmatrix}$

Rule 7: $\text{Mod} \longrightarrow (\text{Perf}) \ (\text{Aux}) \begin{bmatrix} \langle \text{Aspect} \rangle_1 \\ \langle + \text{NOM} \rangle_1 \end{bmatrix} \text{Tns}$

(The other Modal expansions are the same as in chapter 2.)

Rule 8: $\text{Asp} \longrightarrow [+/-\text{Durative}]$

The Verbs will be marked for a specific Aspect feature
in the lexicon, so that the selection of an Aspect
feature applies only to nominalizations, as has been
indicated by the angled brackets. I am limiting my
description to two types of Nominals: Perfective
Nominals, primarily those formed with the suffix <u>ung</u>,

and Durative Nominals, i.e., infinitive Nouns. Thus
[+ Dur] will be identified with the infinitive suffix
[en] and [- Dur] = [+ Perfective] with the suffix [ung].

The first expansion of rule 6 allows for recursive
embedding under NOM. In order to express the
generalization that the Aspect marker enables us to
derive the correct Nominal form I have introduced a
NOM node above the N node. Although I had hoped in
chapter 2 that this node would not have to be in the
tree, I now feel that an intervening NOM node is
needed to express certain generalizations concerning
nominalization in German. The introduction of this
node as well as the form of rule 6 will be justified
in the following section.[2]

4.2.1. Modality fronting in Nominalizations

The introduction of the Modality into our NOM expansion
allows for the expression of another regularity. I
have indicated that there is some support for having
both a Tense and Aspect element present in a nominalized
string. The Tense element will not be realized on the
surface, whereas the Aspect element may eventually
be realized as a particular nominal suffix. Since
the Modality is always the last element in a sentence
we will have to move the nominal suffix--which is

here interpreted as an aspectual marker--into
sentence-second position, so that it can be attached
to the nominal stem. This modality movement, however,
is needed independently to establish the verb-second
position in main clauses.

I have discussed the details of that transformation
both in chapter 3 and in Esau (1971b). At this point
suffice it to point out the similarity of the two
processes involved. The verb-fronting transformation
must be stated to move the two final Modal elements
(e.g., $[HAB + Tns]_{Mod}$) into second position. As I
have stated the nominalization expansion the two
final elements will be $[[Affix]_{Asp} + Tns]_{Mod}$. The
fronting transformation moves the two final elements
in both cases and places them into second position.
In case we have a sentence the Modal elements are
placed immediately after the first NP and in a
nominalization it is placed immediately after NOM.
Thus the fronting rule will look roughly as follows:

SD: X $\begin{Bmatrix} NP \\ NOM \end{Bmatrix}$ Y A + Tns
$\quad\;\;\overline{\quad\quad\quad\quad}\;\;\overline{\quad}\;\;\overline{\quad\quad\quad}$
$\qquad\;\;\; 1 \qquad\qquad 2 \qquad 3$

SC: 1 2 3 $\implies$ 1 3 2

      condition: A is either Aspect or a Verb stem.

4.2.2. <u>Selectional</u> <u>restrictions</u> between <u>Nominals</u> and <u>temporal</u> <u>modifiers</u>

If the aspectual marker is realized as a suffix on
the surface, it must be attached to the preceding
NOM-stem. The tense marker, on the other hand, need
not be realized at the surface; it may, however, be
used to state selectional restrictions between Nominals
and any temporal modifiers associated with them. It
also permits us to state the Tense restrictions for
nominalized embeddings which are a function of the
maxtrix Verb. For example, our grámmar has to generate
sentence (20) as a parallel to sentence (21):

> (20) Ich erfuhr erst jetzt von der gestrigen
>   Ankunft des Erwählten.
>
> (21) Ich erfuhr erst jetzt, dass der Erwählte
>   gestern ankam.

but block the generation of sentences (22) and (23):

> (22) *Ich erfuhr erst jetzt von der morgigen
>   Ankunft des Erwählten.
>
> (23) *Ich erfuhr erst jetzt, dass der Erwählte
>   morgen ankam.

Thus the temporal modifier <u>morgen</u> has to be blocked
both in the <u>dass</u>-complement and in the nominalization.

The presence of a Tense element in both seems to be
the best solution since it expresses at the same time
the similar nature of the constraint. The analysis
of nominalization, as given here, is thus justified
(i) by the formal identity of the two fronting
transformations; (ii) it gives us a simple mechanism
for stating selectional restrictions concerning
temporal modifiers; (iii) it permits us to show that
these selectional restrictions for nominalizations
are of the same kind as for sentential complements,
and (iv) it accounts for the Tense ambiguity found
in nominalized structures.

4.3. Transformationalist vs lexicalist position

In the problem of Nominal derivation in German the
descriptive apparatus provides either for a
transformational or a lexical derivation, whichever
gives a simpler overall-description of the facts of
German. A transformational derivation of a nominalized
structure from its verbal counterpart would capture
the generality, which the speaker of German intuitively
feels, that the following pair of sentences (24) and
(25) are both meaningfully and structurally related:

(24) Er beantwortet die Frage ungenau.

(25) Seine Beantwortung der Frage war ungenau.

However, there are both semantic and syntactic
constraints which complicate a transformational
derivation of sentence (25) from sentence (24). I
shall discuss some of these constraints below.

The second alternative within the transformational
model is the lexicalist position (cf. Chomsky 1965
and Esau (1971c)). This position holds that the
Nominal structure and the one containing its verbal
cognate are only lexically related; the sentences
themselves are generated in the base as separate
structures. The lexicalist position requires that
we express the structural similarity between the
construction (24) and the nominalized part of (25)
by the form of the base rules; the parallelism of
rule 3 and rule 6 is provided with exactly this
purpose in mind. Although the lexicalist position
represents a slight saving in the transformational
component of the grammar, the cost in the lexicon
and the base is obviously greater, for not only must
the second part of the NOM expansion be made an
additional requirement for the lexicalist position
but every Nominal form that could otherwise be derived
by transformation from a cognate Verb must now also
be listed separately in the lexicon.

It is clear that the transformational alternative
is to be preferred, unless it can be shown that there
are irregularities in Nominal/Verb correspondence
which make such an approach too complicated. The
simplicity of the transformational derivation could
not compensate for this, making its adoption impossible.

4.3.1 Lexicalist arguments for UNG-nominals

In Esau (1971c) I have argued that a transformational
derivation is inadequate for the ung-nominals for both
syntactic and semantic reasons while infinitival Nouns
appear to permit a transformational treatment much
more naturally. Contrary to that view I now argue
in the following that the infinitival Nominal must
also be derived lexically. It will be necessary to
summarize my earlier paper briefly.

4.3.1.1. Semantic considerations

The arguments presented there for the lexicalist
derivation of ung-nominals (actually all Nominals
other than infinitival Nouns) were of two kinds:
semantic and syntactic. The semantic problem can be
demonstrated with the following examples:

(26) Jemand wendet (NP) [es behagt ihm nicht].

(27) Die Wendung behagte ihm nicht.

(28) Das Wenden behagte ihm nicht.

(29) Es behagt ihm nicht, dass er wendet.

Sentence (27) may be understood as referring to
Redewendung 'turn of speech', Wendung der Dinge 'turn
of events', Wendung des Weges 'turn of the road' or
'the completed act of turning.' The ung-nominal
appears often to be not only semantically somewhat
removed from its verbal cognate as, e.g., sitzen - Sitzung,
stellen - Stellung, wenden - Wendung, but it may also
have an entirely different semantic range. Sentence (27)
above has, for example, four different interpretations
that are not shared by the other sentences (26, 28, 29).

   These are clearly cases of lexicalization that
cannot be unequivocally predicted, which is characteristic
of lexical items in general. Information of this
sort can only be captured in the lexicon, for the
semantic variations and ambiguities exemplified above
cannot be produced by transformations, if the
transformational component is to represent at all
what Chomsky might call the competence of the
speaker-hearer. An adequate account of the language must
treat these idiosyncratic properties as what they are,
namely lexical properties.

4.3.1.2. Syntactic considerations

The second argument is a syntactic one. I have shown
that gender and number is not predictable in any
consistent manner. In addition, it appears as if
derived Nominals must be marked for syntactic
properties such as [+/- COUNT]. The following examples
are taken from my paper:

(30a) Die Zufriedenheit des Kindes ...

(30b) *Die Zufriedenheiten der Kinder ...

(31a) Jemandem Verlegenheit bereiten ...

(31b) Jemandem Verlegenheiten bereiten.

(32a) Er nimmt jede Gelegenheit wahr.

(32b) Er nimmt alle Gelegenheiten wahr.

(33a) Die Schädlichkeit des Insekts ...

(33b) *Die Schädlichkeiten der Insekten ...

(34a) Die Unbequemlichkeit des Hauses ...

(34b) Die Unbequemlichkeiten des Hauses ...

The feature [+/- COUNT] does not depend on the particular
affix of the Nominal. Although I did not include any
examples of ung-nominals in my earlier paper, the
same holds true for them. Consider the following
examples:

(35a)   Die Verhandlung findet demnächst statt.

(35b)   Die Verhandlungen finden demnächst statt.

(36a)   Die Erholung hatten sie nötig.

(36b)   *Die Erholungen hatten sie nötig.

(37a)   Die Unordnung im Lande ...

(37b)   *Die Unordnungen im Lande ...

(38a)   Die Erhörung seiner Bitte ...

(38b)   *Die Erhörungen seiner Bitten ...

For the starred forms no plural formations are listed in
the dictionary. There is no disagreement among speakers
with regard to plural forms for examples (35-38).
However, for other forms I have noticed a certain amount
of uncertainty among German speakers as to whether
a particular Nominal would ever be used in the plural
or not. There is also some disagreement between
speakers of German and the dictionary entries. For
example, all the speakers questioned agreed that they
would never use the plural of Erziehung, saying that,
if such a form should become necessary, it would be
replaced by Erziehungsysteme or the like. Der
Sprach-Brockhaus (1964:178), on the other hand,
actually lists such a form.[3]

It should be pointed out that the dictionary
entries are often based on whether such a form has
been recorded in the past or not. Such a procedure

obviously does not describe the grammar of German as
a set of rules which the speaker internalizes but
rather as a summation of past occurrences. That is
to say, the dictionary may reflect a former state of
affairs where rules were applied that are no longer
operable. It is understandable that the compilers
of a dictionary have little choice but to make extensive
use of the latter method and this comment is not
intended to be critical. If, however, as in the
case of <u>Erziehung</u> present-day German speakers
unanimously agree that they would not form the plural,
then we must base our description on the intuition
of native speakers rather than on the entries in a
dictionary.

It follows that these derived Nominals, including
the <u>ung</u>-nouns, must be marked for the syntactic
feature [+/- COUNT] in order to eliminate the
ungrammatical strings (36b), (37b), and (38b).

These arguments are sufficient to show that a
transformational derivation of the <u>ung</u>-nominals from
structures containing the corresponding verbal cognates
would not be adequate for a total description of
nominalization in German. There are, of course,
certain syntactic constraints that are shared by both
the nominalization and the corresponding sentence

containing a Verb or Adjective. These constraints, too,
can just as easily, and perhaps even better, be expressed
in the lexicon than by showing their relatedness
in the transformational component. Of course, the
lexicon would have to be sufficiently rich in structure.
Consider now the following strings:

(39a) Die Erfahrung des Mannes ...

(39b) *Die Erfahrung des Hauses ...

(40a) Die Zufriedenheit des Kindes ...

(40b) *Die Zufriedenheit des Buches ...

(41a) Die Verlegenheit des Mannes ...

(41b) Die Verlegenheit der Antwort ...

(42a) Die Unordnung des Mannes ...

(42b) Die Unordnung des Hauses ...

The deep structure for these sentences would be
approximately of the form (T39-42):

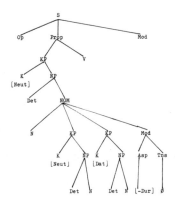

The strings (39a) and (39b) indicate that <u>Erfahrung</u> has

the frame $[+ \text{NOM}, \begin{bmatrix} -\text{DUR} \\ +\text{ung} \end{bmatrix}_{\text{Asp}} \underline{\hspace{1cm}} \text{DAT}]$. <u>Zufriedenheit</u>

has a similar frame except for the affix feature.

<u>Unordnung</u>, on the other hand, has a frame of the form

$[+ \text{NOM}, \begin{bmatrix} -\text{DUR} \\ +\text{ung} \end{bmatrix}_{\text{Asp}} \underline{\hspace{2cm}} (\text{NEUT } \emptyset \text{ DAT})]$. The linked

parentheses indicate that one of two cases must be
chosen but not both. This accounts for the fact that
both (42a) and (42b) are grammatical.

The same constraints hold, however, in the cases
where the verbal or adjectival cognate of the particular
Nominal is used as in the following strings:

(43a)   Der Mann ist erfahren.

(43b)   *Das Haus ist erfahren.

(44a)   Der erfahrene Mann ...

(44b)   *Das erfahrene Haus ...

(45a)   *Das zufriedene Buch ...

(45b)   Das zufriedene Kind ...

(46a)   *Das Buch ist zufrieden.

(46b)   Das Kind ist zufrieden.

(47a)   Der unordentliche Mann ...

(47b)   Das unordentliche Haus ...

(48a)   Das Haus ist unordentlich.

(48b)   Der Mann ist unordentlich.

(49a)   Der Mann ist verlegen.

(49b)   Die Antwort ist verlegen.

(50a)   Die verlegene Antwort ...

(50b)   Der verlegene Mann ...

The constraints noted for Zufriedenheit also hold for
zufrieden; similarly for erfahren and Erfahrung as
well as all the others. This points to the fact that
both zufrieden and Zufriedenheit must have identical
case frames. By showing in the lexicon that both
forms have the same case frame, in spite of their
membership in different syntactic categories, we have
expressed a generalization that appears only
accidental if (39a) were derived transformationally
from (43a). Thus the parallelism of their case frames
supports the lexicalist rather than the transformationali
position.

　　　The distributional similarity becomes even clearer
if we choose a noun such as Überzeugung which can have
two different case frames as demonstrated by the
following examples:

(51a)   Die Überzeugung des Mannes ...

(51b)   Die Überzeugung des Freundes $\begin{Bmatrix} \text{durch den Mann} \\ \text{mit dem Buch} \end{Bmatrix}$

(51c)   Der Mann überzeugt den Freund (mit dem Buch).

(51d)   Das Buch überzeugt den Freund.

(51e)   Der Mann ist überzeugt (hat eine Überzeugung).

The deep structure of sentence (51c) could be represented
as in (T51c):

(T51c)

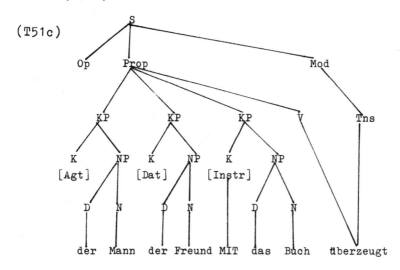

In the case of nominalization only the Dative NP
may be raised into a surface Genitive as in string (51b).
The nominalization (51a), however, cannot be derived from
the same deep structure (T51c); although it may appear
so superficially, (51a) is not the result of raising
the Agentive NP der Mann of (T51c) to the surface
Genitive. It is rather the same Dative NP which we
find as Subject of sentence (51e). The optional
Instrumental NP das Buch of (T51c) may not be raised

to surface Genitive either although it can become
the Subject of the verbal construction (51d). This,
however, is due to general constraints on genitivizing
in nominalizations.[4]

Überzeugen as used in (51c) and (51d) has the
frame [+ VERB _____ (AGT ◊ INSTR) DAT]. However,
only the Nominal Überzeugung in (51b) has this frame
$[+ \text{NOM} \begin{bmatrix} -\text{DUR} \\ +\text{ung} \end{bmatrix}$ _____ (AGT ◊ INSTR) DAT]. Überzeugung
in string (51a), on the other hand, has the case frame
$[+ \text{NOM,} \begin{bmatrix} -\text{DUR} \\ +\text{ung} \end{bmatrix}$ _____ DAT] parallel to überzeugt in
sentence (51e): $\begin{bmatrix} \begin{bmatrix} +\text{VERB} \\ -\text{V} \end{bmatrix} & \text{_____ DAT} \end{bmatrix}$. $\begin{bmatrix} +\text{VERB} \\ +\text{V} \end{bmatrix}$ is
used to mark Adjectives whereas Verbs are redundantly
marked as $\begin{bmatrix} +\text{VERB} \\ +\text{V} \end{bmatrix}$.

Although it is clear that the verbal/nominal
correspondence must be captured in an adequate
description of the language, it has again become
apparent from the last examples that this can be
accomplished much more easily in the lexicon than in
the transformational component. If the various forms
are related in the lexicon, there will be four
subentries under the lexical prime ÜBERZEUG (cf. the
next section for a more detailed description of

lexical entries.) Under the Perfective Nominal entry
two frames are listed and under [+ VERB] the same
two frames appear, thus relating one [+ NOM] entry
to the $\begin{bmatrix} +\text{VERB} \\ + \text{ V} \end{bmatrix}$ form and the other to the $\begin{bmatrix} +\text{VERB} \\ - \text{ V} \end{bmatrix}$ form
by the identity of their associated case frames.

4.3.2. Lexicalist arguments for infinitival Nouns

Let us now turn to the infinitival Nouns. In my earlier
paper I argued that infinitival nominalization is a
transformational process; i.e., sentence (52a) is
related to (52b) by transformation rather than in the
lexicon.

> (52a) [[Sein Erzählen der Geschichte] wirkte
> langweilig].
> (52b) Er erzählte die Geschichte.

This decision was based both on syntactic and on
semantic arguments.

4.3.2.1. Semantic considerations

Semantically it is apparent that all infinitival Nouns
are consistently perceived as [+ Durative], which is a
quality that one would expect with Verbs rather than
with Nouns. This fact seemed to suggest a transformational

treatment of infinitive Nouns. The latter also do
not show the unpredictable semantic range of, e.g.,
the ung-nominals. In fact the semantic interpretation
of infinitive Nouns relates rather closely to that
of the cognate Verbs. A transformational derivation
of infinitival Nouns from an underlying structure
containing its verbal cognate would thus create no
problems for the semantic interpretations of the
resulting surface structures.

4.3.2.2. Syntactic considerations

Secondly, let us look at the syntactic arguments. I
noted in my paper that the infinitive Nouns are totally
productive. When Chomsky (1967) introduced the
criterion of productivity he did not define it
unambiguously, for it referred both to the fact that
certain Nominals can be derived from every Verb or
Adjective in the language and to the fact that these
Nominals occur in the same syntactic environments as
the corresponding Verb or Adjective does. In my
earlier paper I was primarily concerned with the first
sense of productivity. This induced me to give only
superficial attention to the second sense, i.e.,
productivity with regard to syntactic environments.
The first sense of productivity is clearly matched

by the German infinitival Nouns. Although there may
be individual exceptions, as I shall show in the next
section, our grammar must also derive an infinitival
Nominal for the greater number of German Verbs.
Consider these three examples from my earlier paper:

(53a)　Peter singt ein Lied.

(53b)　Peters Singen des Liedes ...

(54a)　Er schnarcht jede Nacht ...

(54b)　Sein Schnarchen jede Nacht ...

(55a)　Er zerstört die Stadt.

(55b)　Sein Zerstören der Stadt ...

The second sense of productivity, however, is
much more relevant for deciding whether these Nominals
are to be derived through transforms or are to be
introduced as base structures. With regard to this
second sense, a reanalysis of the facts has shown that
my earlier claim--that infinitival Nouns may be
derived through transforms--is untenable and should
be modified.

There are, of course, syntactic restrictions
which are not noun-like properties in general,
particularly the predictability of gender and number,
which holds for all infinitive Nouns in the language.
All infinitival Nouns are inherently Neuter and can

only be used in the Singular. However, certain
restrictions upon a particular gender are apparent
for other derived Nouns as well (e.g., the ung-nominals
are exclusively Feminine). This peculiarity of
infinitival Nouns must not necessarily be attributed
to the fact that they are related to Verbs. The
constraint that limits Nouns to Singular can be just
as adequately accounted for when the Durative Nominal
analysis is assumed, for it is not surprising at all
that Nominals which express a duration rather than
a perfective or abstracted state resist being counted.
By analyzing these Nouns as Duratives, the [- COUNT]
character of these forms can be attributed to their
particular aspectual content and thus naturally
explained.

Infinitival Nouns do not permit the same range
of complementizers that their corresponding Verbs do,
as the following strings show:

(56a) Ich weiss, dass er zu Hause ist.

(56b) Er schreibt, dass er morgen zurückkommt.

(56c) Das Kind schreit, damit es gehört wird.

(56d) Er braucht das Buch nicht zu lesen.

(57a) *Mein Wissen, dass er zu Hause ist ...

(57b) *Sein Schreiben, dass er morgen zurückkommt ..

(57c)*Das Schreien das Kindes, damit es gehört wird ..

(57d)*Sein Brauchen, das Buch (des Buches) nicht

      zu lesen ...

(58a)*Seine Schrift, dass er morgen zurückkommt ...

(58b)*Der Schrei des Kindes, damit es gehört wird ..

Neither the derived Nouns of the type: <u>Schrei</u>,
<u>Schrift</u> nor the infinitival Nouns permit the
complementizers that occur with the corresponding Verbs.
This strongly suggests that infinitival Nouns too
are to be introduced as base structures, in which case
these constraints must be stated in the lexicon.

The infinitival Nouns share other syntactic
features that seem to group them with the other derived
Nouns in the lexicon. If the restrictions concerning
number and gender are ignored, infinitive Nouns share
with the latter a similar range of determiner selection
as the following examples show:

(59a)   Ein Singen des Liedes kam nicht in Frage.

(59b)   Jedes erneute Singen des Liedes trug zur
       Stimmung bei.

(59c)   Alles Singen half nichts.

(59d)   Jenes Singen hat sogar meinem Vater gefallen.

(59e)   Dein Singen klang ausgezeichnet.

Infinitival Nouns permit relativization just
as other derived Nouns. There is, however, an essential
distinction between the way infinitival Nominals
relativize and the way others do, which I shall discuss
in the following section. At this point it suffices
to point out that infinitival Nouns relativize as do
those Nouns which are clearly lexically derived. If,
on the other hand, the structure with the corresponding
Verb is relativized, the result is an ungrammatical
string:

(60a)   Der Gesang, den ich hörte, ...

(60b)   Das Singen, das ich hörte ...

(60c)   *Jemand sang, das ich hörte.

Thus, the syntactic arguments above strongly suggest
that infinitival Nouns should be introduced as base
structures rather than as transforms from structures
with the corresponding Verbs.

4.3.3. Hartung's transformationalist analysis

Hartung's (1964) description of some aspects of
nominalizations in German represents an interesting
attempt to derive Nominals transformationally from
sentences. Hartung observes a number of very

interesting restrictions on the derivation of Nominals
without, however, being able to integrate these
constraints into an optimal description of Nominal
processes. I shall briefly show how the facts presented
by Hartung can be easily accounted for if the lexicalist
position advocated here is adopted. The nominalization
referred to by Hartung (1964:55 ff.) as <u>substantivische
Nominalisierung</u> includes, among others, the two types
of Nominals treated in this chapter. Hartung points
out that a nominalization is in general possible
if the Verb is intransitive as:

> (61)   Der Mann kommt ⟶
>   Das Kommen des Mannes ... [1]

He further notices that there are certain restrictions
necessary for transitive Verbs in order to prevent
the derivation of ungrammatical strings:

(i) Nominalizations are usually possible if the
    Verb takes only one or more Prepositional
    Phrases. Thus (62) is grammatical:

> (62)   Der Autor ärgert sich über die Kritiker ⟶
>   Der Ärger des Autors über die Kritiker. [8]

(ii) The nominalization, however, becomes
    ungrammatical as soon as the sentence contains

an additional Accusative, Dative, or Genitive
surface Object not introduced by a Preposition
as in:

(63) Die Polizei verhaftet einen Verbrecher ⟶
      *Die Verhaftung der Polizei einen Verbrecher
      (or des Verbrechers). [9]

(iii) Sentences like (63), however, become grammatical
as soon as the passive sentence is taken as
the input to the nominalization transformation:

(64) Ein Verbrecher wurde durch die Polizei
      verhaftet ⟶
      die Verhaftung eines Verbrechers
      durch die Polizei. [17]

(iv)   Nominalization appears to be possible from
an active sentence containing an additional
Accusative Object if the Agent NP is realized
as a possessive. Thus we can derive:

(65) ihre Verhaftung eines Verbrechers. [15]

(v)   If both an Agent and an Object NP is present
a nominalization is possible only if the
Object NP is deleted during the derivational
process. Thus, by eliminating the Object NP

we derive:

>   (66)   Die Beanstandung des Kunden ist
>   berechtigt.

In the last example the complete sentence
must be understood as:

>   (66') Die Beanstandung des Kunden (von etwas)
>   ist berechtigt.

4.3.4. Reanalysis of Hartung's observations

4.3.4.1. Restrictions on genitivization in nominalized structures

I believe that all of these facts have one explanation
in common and can be formulated in one general rule.
Only an NP that is not introduced by a Preposition can
be genitivized, which limits the genitivizable NP's
to what is here referred to as Agentive, Dative, and
Neutral NP's. The Agentive NP is included among the
NP's that need not be introduced by a Preposition,
although it appears in the deep structure with the
Agentive Preposition VON in the tree. However, this
Preposition becomes deleted if the Agent NP is
selected as Subject of the sentence, or if the Agent NP
is genitivized. I.e., only if the Agent NP is forced
out of its sentence-first position by another NP must

the Preposition be realized on the surface.

The second limitation that must be incorporated
into the SD of the genitivization rule is that no
genitivization is possible if there are at least two
NP's present in a string which are not introduced by
a Preposition in the way just described. There are
obviously a number of ways in which a second
unintroduced NP can be eliminated. One way would be
to apply the possessive transformation which converts
either an Agent or a Dative NP into a possessive
Adjective.[5]

Possessives will be generated in two ways:
inalienable possession starts out as an S under the
Det of the KP which it modifies. Alienable possession,
on the other hand, starts out under the Dative KP
and is then attached to the Det node of the NP showing
possession. Thus, after the possessive rule has
applied, all possessive adjective stems will be attached
to the Det node of the NP they modify. The possessives
modifying nominalizations, which can come from either
an Agent or a Dative KP, are treated in the same
manner as inalienable possession. One justification
for this procedure is that possessives with Nominals
are often structurally ambiguous. For example,

(67)   sein Dank

can come from either one of the two underlying structures

(68)   Er dankt jemandem.

(69)   Jemand dankt ihm.

depending on the context.   Besides generating sentences
of the type

(70)   Seine Kündigung des Vertrags

the possessive rule also generates strings like (71)

(71)   Karls Kündigung des Vertrags

where the Proper Noun takes the place of the possessive
adjective.   Since only Proper Nouns can occur in this
position the possessive rule could apply to either NP's
marked as $\begin{bmatrix} +\text{Pro} \\ +\text{Possess} \end{bmatrix}$ or to NP's where the Noun is
marked [+ Proper].

The possessive transformation, therefore, must
be ordered before the genitivizing transformation
that applies to nominalized structures.   In this way
possessives and Proper Nouns have already become
attached to the Det node of the NP to be possessivized
and do not interfere with the genitivizing
transformation.

Another way to dispose of NP's would be to delete
an indefinite Neutral NP. This rule, too, has to
precede the genitivizing rule. A third way would be
to start from a passive sentence, to speak with Hartung.
However, this complication is necessary only in a
grammar that attempts to derive the passive from the
active counterpart. Since in the case model active
and passive sentences are derived independently from
the same underlying tree the problem of whether a
genitivization should take the active or the passive
sentence as its source is nonexistent. If it should
turn out that the constraint on the genitivizing rule
can be stated just as easily without reference to the
passive sentence, this approach would be preferable.

However, these facts can also be explained in
a different way, without the assumption that
genitivization operates on passive sentences. We will
interpret constraint (iii) above as a restriction on
the number of NP's not introduced by Prepositions,
which is essentially in agreement with constraints (i)
and (ii). I.e., only one NP without an expressed
prepositional head may be present for the genitivizing
rule to be operative. We have seen above that the Agent
NP is always introduced by a Preposition if it is not
selected as Subject of the sentence. A nominalization

containing both an Agentive and Neutral NP will,thus,
always meet the structural description of the
genitivizing rule, if the Neutral NP is genitivized.
The fact that in the corresponding sentence the Neutral
NP would become the Subject (i.e., a passive sentence
is generated) should, of course, be expressed in some way.

4.3.4.2. Rules of object fronting

For our description to be adequate, we should expect
that this parallelism is expressable by the similarity
of the respective rules. It should perhaps even be
possible to conflate the passive rule applying to
sentences and the genitivizing rule applying to
nominalizations.

   The passive transformation simply takes a Neutral
or Dative NP and interchanges it with the Agent NP.
Whenever a Neutral is present, it must be chosen
as the Subject NP. Bierwisch (1963) and others have
suggested that the order of NP's should be, in our
terms, Agentive, Dative and Neutral, because of the
permutation rules; the passive rule, however, indicates
that this order is not the best since it would complicate
the passive considerably. We shall see below that
the genitivization rule provides evidence for the same
fact. To judge from these two instances the order must

rather be <u>Agentive</u>, <u>Neutral</u>, <u>Dative</u>. It needs to be
seen if the rest of the grammar will support this
ordering proposal. If the first order were assumed,
we would need the following SD for the passive rule:

$$\text{SD:} \quad \underline{X} \quad \underline{\text{Agt}^{[KP]}} \quad \underline{\text{Dat}^{[KP]}} \quad \underline{\text{Neut}^{[KP]}} \quad \underline{Y} \quad \underline{\begin{bmatrix} \text{WERD} \\ \text{+Pass} \end{bmatrix}} \quad \underline{Z}$$
$$\quad\;\; 1 \qquad 2 \qquad\;\; 3 \qquad\quad 4 \quad\;\; 5 \qquad 6 \qquad\;\; 7$$

it would be extremely difficult to state that both
the Dative and the Neutral KP are optional yet <u>one must</u>
be present for the rule to apply, but that the Neutral
<u>must</u> be selected when present. Assuming the second
order the SD and SC can be stated as follows:

$$\text{SD:} \quad X \quad \underline{\text{Agt}^{[KP]}} \quad \underline{\text{Neut}^{[KP]} \quad \text{Dat}^{[KP]}} \quad Y \quad \underline{\begin{bmatrix} \text{WERD} \\ \text{+Pass} \end{bmatrix}} \quad Z$$
$$\underline{\;}\quad\;\; \underline{\quad\;} \qquad \underline{\qquad\qquad\;} \quad\;\; \underline{\;} \quad \underline{\quad\;} \quad \underline{\;}$$
$$\;\; 1 \qquad 2 \qquad\qquad\;\; 3 \qquad\quad 4 \quad\;\; 5 \qquad 6$$

$$\text{SC:} \quad 1 \;\; 2 \;\; 3 \;\; 4 \;\; 5 \;\; 6 \implies 1 \;\; 3 \;\; 2 \;\; 4 \;\; 5 \;\; 6$$

Condition: Dative and Neutral are optional but
one has to be present.

This will ensure that the Neutral NP is always in
sentence-first position and that the Dative NP can
only become Subject of a passive sentence if no
Neutral NP is present. The passive <u>WERD</u> has already

been introduced with the base rules as shown in chapter 3.

The genitivization transformation consists of two parts. It may be stated as follows:

Genitivization T. Part 1:

SD: X $_{Agt}[KP]$ $_{Neut}[KP]$ $_{Dat}[KP]$ Y $[^{N}_{+NOM}]$ Z

— ———— ————————— — ——— —

1   2   3   4   5   6

SC: 1 2 3 4 5 6 $\Longrightarrow$ 1 3 2 4 5 6

Condition: Dative and Neutral are optional but only one may occur in a string.

This rule is obligatory in that a string meeting the SD must undergo the rule. It is, however, optional with respect to the second part of the genitivization rule. I.e., a string may undergo part 2 of the genitivization rule without having undergone part 1.

Part 2 of the genitivization rule involves the actual introduction of the genitive marker into the first NP of a nominalized string and the fronting of the nominalized form.

Genitivization T.   Part 2:

SD: X   NP   Y   N
                        [+NOM]
      $\overline{1}$ $\overline{2}$ $\overline{3}$ $\overline{4}$

SC: 1   2   3   4 $\Longrightarrow$ 1   4   2   3
                                              [+Gen]

There is some indication that part 1 and 2 of the
genitivization transformation should be treated
separately and not as one rule. First of all the
assignment of the surface Genitive to the first NP
can and should probably be done in the surface case
assignment rules. I am not sure at this point when
the nominalized Noun has to be fronted and shall,
therefore, leave the question open here.

Much stronger evidence for treating part 1 of
the genitivization transformation separately comes
from the fact that this rule can easily be conflated
with the passive transformation which selects the
Subject of a passive sentence. If these two rules
are conflated, we may simply regard the rule as an
object fronting transformation, whereby in one case
the object fronting is conditioned by the feature
[+ Passive] and in the other case by the feature
[+ Nominal].[6] The object fronting transformation may
now be stated as:

SD: $X \quad _{Agt}[KP] \quad _{Neut}[KP] \quad _{Dat}[KP] \quad Y \left\{ \begin{bmatrix} \begin{bmatrix} WERD \\ [+Pass] \end{bmatrix} \\ \begin{bmatrix} N \\ [+NOM] \end{bmatrix} \end{bmatrix} \right\} Z$

$$\underline{} \quad \underline{} \quad \underline{} \quad \underline{} \quad \underline{} \quad \underline{}$$

$$1 \qquad 2 \qquad\qquad 3 \qquad\qquad 4 \qquad 5 \qquad 6$$

SC: $1 \quad 2 \quad 3 \quad 4 \quad 5 \quad 6 \implies 1 \quad 3 \quad 2 \quad 4 \quad 5 \quad 6$

Condition: <u>Dative</u> and <u>Neutral</u> are optional but

(i) if $\begin{bmatrix} WERD \\ [+Pass] \end{bmatrix}$ occurs in the string both may be present,

(ii) if $\begin{bmatrix} N \\ [+NOM] \end{bmatrix}$ occurs in the string only one may be present,

(iii) if $\begin{bmatrix} WERD \\ [+Pass] \end{bmatrix}$ occurs in the string the rule is optional,

(iv) if $\begin{bmatrix} N \\ [+NOM] \end{bmatrix}$ occurs in the string the rule is obligatory.

If in a nominalized string no Dative or Neutral NP is present, the Agent NP will be genitivized automatically, i.e., the rule applies vacuously. For example:

(72) Die Kündigung des Beamten ...

I have ignored so far cases where the nominalization requires a certain Preposition for a following KP but the corresponding Verb does not, for example,

Hartung's pair:

> (73) Peter dankt seinem Freund.
>
>   Peters Dank an seinen Freund.

How this information might be introduced in a
transformational framework is not clear to me. It seems
that the lexicon is the proper place to state such
idiosyncracies. And this is exactly what the lexicalist
proposal entails.

I shall conclude this section by indicating the
relative order of the rules discussed above:

> 1. possessive transformation
>
> 2. indefinite object NP deletion transformation
>
> 3. object fronting transformation

Rule 1 and 2 do not seem to be ordered with respect
to one another. But both must precede the object
fronting rule as stated here.

5. INFINITIVAL AND UNG-NOMINALS

5.1. <u>Preliminary</u> <u>remarks</u>

In this section I analyze two types of German
Nominals, the group of Nominals formed with the
derivational suffix <u>ung</u> and the infinitival Nouns.
While it is desirable to relate both groups of Nominals,
either transformationally or lexically, to their
verbal cognates in the grammar, I have shown in the
preceding section that a transformational derivation
is not plausible. This means that within the
transformational model, the lexicon is the only place
where the relationships of these Nouns to their verbal
cognates can be made explicit. Since the similarity
of their structural description has been provided for
in the base rules, the derivation of the verbal and
nominal forms need no longer be attributed to their
derivation from a single underlying form.

Investigation of those Verbs that allow the
ung-formation and those that do not indicates that
the speaker of German does not learn each form as a
separate lexical item, but acquires these Nominals
by some general process which leads to uniform output
and agreement among speakers as to which Verbs permit
the ung-formation and which do not. Except for some
borderline cases, all speakers appear to agree on which
ung-nominals are grammatical and which are not. This
fact suggests strongly that the formation of Nominals
with the derivational suffix ung- is not merely a
matter of chance, but is, in fact, entirely predictable.

5.2. The lexical function of UNG

A survey of Verbs for which the ung-formation is not
possible shows clearly that it would be a futile
undertaking to try to find any one single feature
that would make it possible to group all of these
forms into a natural class. The following random
selection of Verbs, none of which has an ung-nominalization, gives an idea of the problem:

   haben, danken, fliehen, gehen, kochen, leiden,
   heissen, kennen, lassen, gelingen, donnern,
   beschliessen, singen, brüten, anrufen,

    einfallen, stehlen, erschrecken, schweigen,
    frieren, geben, fallen, beweisen, etc.

Since no single feature or even a small set of features
can be determined for the placing of these Verbs into
a natural class which will distinguish them
unmistakably from Verbs allowing ung-nominalization,
it is necessary to look further for the reason that
these Verbs lack this sort of nominalization. Since
the Verbs themselves do not indicate why this should
be so--unless one assumes this to be purely the result
of historical accident--one must ask what the function
of these ung-nominals might be in the German Nominal
system, if they were to exist.

     Ung has been identified in chapter 3 as a perfective
suffix, so that the ung-nominals may be regarded as
Perfective Nouns. Consider the Durative Verb zerstören
in

    (1) Er zerstört die Stadt.

If the inflected Verb is nominalized and replaced by
Zerstörung the implication is that the act of destroying
is viewed with the end-point in mind, whether this
end-point has been realized at the moment of speaking
or not. Zerstörung is thus inherently Perfective
with regard to the way in which it views the action.

This remains independent of whether or not it already belongs to the past, for Aspect and Tense are separate and unrelated parameters in verbal forms.

It depends to a large degree on the rest of the sentence whether the Perfective Aspect actually predominates in the surface realization of the sentence. This, however, does not primarily concern my argument. It is, not difficult to construct a sentence in which the predominant Aspect differs from that which is inherent in the Nominal itself, e.g.:

(2)   Der Feind wiederholte die Zerstörung der
       Stadt immer wieder.

In this sentence the predominant Aspect seems to be Aorist. It may also be argued that some ung-nouns, as, e.g., die Hoffnung are not Perfective at all, as I have claimed, since hope obviously pertains to the future. This is, however, only an incomplete analysis of the facts. It is not the realization of hope that is at stake--which is a matter of Tense--but rather whether it is viewed with an end-point in mind where the thing hoped for has been entirely conceptualized, i.e., has become perfected. Thus, when the speaker uses the Nominal Hoffnung instead of the Durative Noun das Hoffen, he views the action with this end-point of conceptualization in mind.

Let us, therefore, assume that the _ung_-derivations
are in all cases Perfective Nouns according to my
definition.[1] Should there be some exceptions to
this general rule, the forms would be marked individually
in the lexicon. It seems reasonable to assume that
this would indeed represent an idiosyncratic feature
of those exceptional forms, so that we would be required
to represent this information in the lexicon in any
case.

By way of digression, I shall now extend Fillmore's
notion of grammatical functions. Just as there are
certain semantically based case functions such that
we may think of individual deep case categories as
functional slots that are necessary for the communication
process, there are other grammatical functions as well.
For example, let us assume that language L has one
hundred Verb entries in its lexicon to express one
hundred different actions and states. Let us further
assume that one of the Verb entries is the Verb to give.
It would be unusual if L did not also have a way of
expressing the completed act of giving or the thing
being given. The same is true for all the other Verbs
in L. Thus there are certain functional slots in the
lexicon which the speaker of L expects to be filled.[2]

Every speaker has at one time or another hunted
for a certain word; he may even have indicated that
he needs a lexical item to express a certain notion,
or--to state it in my terminology--to fill a particular
slot in the language. For example, if speaker A
wanted to express the notion <u>capable of being read</u>
he would find in the lexicon the form <u>readable</u>. If
he wanted to express the notion <u>capable of being seen</u>
he may again scan the lexicon and after trying the form
<u>*seeable</u> find the form <u>visible</u> as one of the possible
entries. In the case of some verbs, e.g., <u>to ask</u>,
<u>to stand up</u>, his search for the notion <u>capable of being</u>
... would only produce the questionable if not totally
ungrammatical forms <u>*askable</u> and <u>*stand-up-able</u>. This
would force him to paraphrase it in some other way.

5.3. <u>Perfective Nominal slot</u>

Let us now return to our discussion of <u>ung</u>-nominals
in German and assume that it is desirable from the
point of view of the speaker to have a Perfective
Nominal cognate for every Verb in the lexicon. Should
it turn out that the great majority of Verbs follow
this pattern, we may consider there to be a lexical
class within the grammar of the German speaker whose
function may be called the Perfective Nominal function.

We will assume that there exists a slot in this
Perfective Nominal class corresponding to every Verb
in the lexicon. Since all ung-nominals are here
considered to be Perfective Nouns they would be
expected to fill this slot.

From this point it is only one logical step to
the assumption that the reason a particular Verb
does not permit the ung-derivation is the fact that
this slot is already filled by another Perfective Noun.
It may be this phenomenon which causes uncertainty
among speakers of German wherever another Perfective
Noun exists for a particular lexical form, whether
the ung-formation is grammatical.

5.3.1. Nominals without UNG

In the list below I have created a number of ung-nominals
from Verbs that apparently do not permit this nominalization.
Next to each form I have entered, wherever possible,
the corresponding Perfective Noun or Nouns which seem
to fill the Perfective Nominal slot for a particular
verbal cognate. Note that I am making the claim that
the relationship between a Verb and the corresponding
Perfective Noun is part of the native speaker's
competence and that the speaker is fully aware of the

fact that a Verb and its Nominal cognate belong together
and can easily produce the Nominal form when he is
provided with a particular Verb. I have actually
tested this with a number of native speakers. After
some help on the first two forms, they were generally
able to respond rapidly with the corresponding Nominal.
I consider this fact to be a confirmation of my
contention.

*Anfangung	Anfang
*Anrufung	Anruf
*Arbeitung	Arbeit
*Aufrufung	Aufruf
*Ausruhung	Ruhe
*Badung	Bad
*Beginnung	Beginn
*Begreifung	Begriff
*Bellung	Gebell
*Beschliessung	Beschluss
*Beweisung	Beweis
*Blitzung	Blitz
*Brauchung	Gebrauch
*Brütung	Brut
*Dankung	Dank
*Dauerung	Dauer

*Denkung	Gedanke
*Donnerung	Donner
*Drückung	Druck
*Dürstung	Durst
*Eilung	Eile
*Empfangung	Empfang
*Erlebung	Erlebnis
*Essung	Essen
*Findung	Fund
*Fragung	Frage
*Freuung	Freude
*Frierung	Frost
*Fürchtung	Furcht
*Gefallung	Gefallen
*Gehörung	Besitz
*Greifung	Griff
*Grüssung	Gruss
*Haglung	Hagel
*Hassung	Hass
*Heiratung	Heirat
*Heissung ⎫ *Nennung ⎭	Name
*Helfung	Hilfe
*Hörung	Gehör
*Jagung	Jagd

*Kämmung	Kamm
*Kennung	Kunde
*Klingung	Klang
*Kostung	Kost
*Lachung	Gelächter
*Lassung	Nachlass
*Lebung	Leben
*Leidung	Leid
*Lesung	Lese
*Leuchtung	Licht
*Liegung	Lage
*Lügung	Lüge
*Nähung	Naht
*Ratung	Rat
*Rauchung	Rauch
*Reissung	Riss
*Riechung	Geruch
*Rufung	Ruf
*Scheinung	Schein
*Schlafung	Schlaf
*Schlagung	Schlag
*Schliessung	Schluss
*Schreibung	Schrift
*Schreiung	Schrei
*Schweigung	Schweigen

*Sehung	Sicht
*Singung	Gesang
*Sprechung	Sprache
*Stehlung	Diebstahl
*Stehung	Stand
*Sterbung	Tod
*Stürzung	Sturz
*Tragung	Last
*Treffung	Treffen
*Tretung	Tritt
*Trinkung	Trank
*Tuung	Tat
*Verbietung	Verbot
*Verlierung	Verlust
*Verstehung	Verstand
*Vorschlagung	Vorschlag
*Wachsung	Wuchs
*Wachung	Wacht
*Waschung	Wäsche
*Werfung	Wurf
*Wissung	Wissen
*Zeigung	Zeichen
*Zielung	Ziel

Sein-verbs:

*Bleibung	Bleibe
*Einfallung	Einfall
*Erschreckung	Schreck
*Ertrinkung	Tod durch Ertrinken
*Fahrung	Fahrt
*Fallung	Fall
*Fliegung	Flug
*Fliehung	Flucht
*Fliessung	Fluss
*Flüchtung	Flucht
*Gehung	Gang
*Gelingung	Erfolg
*Geschehung	Geschehen
*Kommung ⎱	
*Ankommung ⎰	Ankunft
*Sinkung	Untergang ?
*Springung	Sprung
*Steigung	Aufstieg
*Verschwindung	Schwund

Modals:

*Dürfung	Erlaubnis
*Habung	Habe
*Könnung	?

*Müssung	Muss
*Seiung	Sein
*Sollung	Soll
*Werdung	?
*Wollung	Wille

Verbs of exchange:

*Borgung	?
*Bringung	?
*Gebung	? (Gabe)
*Holung	?
*Leihung	?
*Nehmung	?

5.3.2. Apparent and real exceptions

For most forms it is fairly easy for a native speaker
to come up with the corresponding Perfective Noun.
However, there are a few exceptions which fall into
at least three groups.

For a few Verbs it is impossible to construct a
Nominal cognate where the verbal stem is still
recognizable. Among these are the following Verbs:

gehören	schweigen
gelingen	sterben
heissen	tragen

Although no ung-forms are permitted for these Verbs,
there seem to be no stem-related Perfective Nouns
in the language. However, if the notion that these
cognates must be formally similar is disregarded--although
this is for the most part true--and they are conceived
rather in terms of their function in the total grammar,
the native speaker will generally agree on the particular
Noun which fills any particular slot. The following
pairing, therefore, will hardly ever cause disagreement
among speakers of German:

*Gelingung	Erfolg
*Sterbung	Tod
*Gehörung	Besitz (Hort)
*Heissung	Name
*Tragung	Last
*Ertrinkung	Tod durch Ertrinken

This analysis suggests that Erfolg fills the slot
of the Perfective Noun cognate to the Verb gelingen,
Tod takes the place of *Sterbung and so on. All these
Nouns, which have taken over the function of the
ung-nominals, with the exception of Erfolg and Besitz,
do not have a verbal cognate; this fact gives some
additional support to my explanation. Although
erfolgen is formally related to Erfolg, it is clear

that the relationship of the two forms is historical
and would probably not be recognized by the speaker,
who would be much more inclined to relate Erfolg
to gelingen than to the semantically very different
erfolgen. Besitz on the other hand does have a verbal
cognate besitzen, which, however, is so similar to
gehören that Besitz can easily be perceived as being
the Perfective Nominal for both of these Verbs.
Besitzen and gehören differ only in the element to be
topicalized, i.e., the element that appears as the
surface Subject. Besitzen normally topicalizes the
one that possesses and gehören the thing possessed.
In the case of the Nominal such a distinction is, of
course, impossible which accounts for the presence
of only one form.

As a Perfective Nominal for the non-existent
Ertrinkung, Tod durch Ertrinken may seem to be strained
at first, but this is the circumlocution a German
speaker would normally use if he wanted to express
the Perfective state of having died by drowning.
Thus, it seems reasonable to assume that this somewhat
awkward expression fills the slot of *Ertrinkung.

The second group of exceptions consists of those
in which one Nominal apparently fulfills the Perfective
Nominal function for two verbal cognates, one with

and the other without a particular prefix; e.g., <u>die</u>
<u>Ankunft</u> fills the Perfective Noun slot for both <u>kommen</u>
and <u>ankommen</u>. This is not surprising, however, when
the earlier definition of <u>Perfective</u>[3] is taken into
consideration. The Perfective form that corresponds
to the Durative <u>kommen</u> is by definition identical to
<u>ankommen</u>, so that the existence of only one form for
both Verbs is a natural consequence. There is then no
need in the language for another Perfective Nominal
cognate with <u>kommen</u>.

The third group of <u>exceptions</u> in our sample
contains true exceptions. It includes the following
Verbs:

bringen	—	holen
nehmen	—	geben
leihen	—	borgen
schenken, schicken	—	bekommen.[4]

The <u>ung</u>-nominalization rule does not apply to these
Verbs, traditionally referred to as <u>Verbs of exchange</u>.
A survey of the lexicon reveals that there are no
corresponding Perfective Nouns in the language at
all for these Verbs. Linguists have long recognized
that Verbs of exchange because of their frequent use
are subject to special developments in many languages.

It is quite significant, therefore, that these Verbs
have no corresponding Perfective Nouns in the lexicon.
Leihen - borgen, bringen - holen and so on are pairs
which express complementary oppositions. Gabe and
Geschenk may be considered the Perfective Nominals
for geben and schenken. But they are almost entirely
associated with the objects given, with hardly any
reference to the action of giving itself. Gabe can
also have the Perfective Nominal interpretation in a
somewhat abstract sense as in (3):

(3) Er hat die Gabe, alles zu behalten.

Apart from these two cases a regular pattern emerges
even here. Verbs of exchange could then be marked
with some feature like [+ Exchange] and we could
stipulate that none of these Verbs is related to a
corresponding Perfective Nominal so that they cannot
undergo the ung-nominalization rule.

Other generalizations can obviously be made about
Verbs which do not permit ung-nominalization. Modals
form a natural class of Verbs that belong to this
category. Another is the group of Verbs traditionally
called sein-verbs. A third group comprises the Verbs
of sense perception.

5.3.3. Nominals with UNG

Next let us look at those Verbs that allow the
ung-formation. The following quote from Schulz-Griesbach
is representative of the treatment of these Nominals
in traditional grammars. We read (1965:14) '-ung:
bildet FEMININE NOMEN aus Verben, sehr häufig aus
Verben mit Präfixen'. This description is followed
by a list of ten Nouns with ung-suffixes. No more
is said about these Nominals. When what has here been
said about non-existent ung-forms is taken into account,
it is clear that more can and must be said about the
ung-nominals. The following list contains a number
of ung-nominals. Alongside we have placed other
Perfective Nouns which are--historically at least--related
to the same verbal cognate:

Ausarbeitung

Begrenzung

Behandlung

Besinnung

Entdeckung

Entstehung

Erfahrung

Erforschung

Erlernung

Ermittlung

Erwartung

Fahndung

Hoffnung

Lösung

Meinung

Sitzung

Überlegung

Vergebung

Verhandlung

Verleumdung

Wahrnehmung

Wanderung

Wohnung

Zahlung

Zeugung

Zumutung

Berufung	–	Beruf
Beziehung	–	Bezug
Handlung	–	Handel
Vorsehung	–	Vorsicht
Ziehung	–	Zug

Most Nominals in <u>ung</u> represent the only Perfective
Nouns corresponding to a particular Verb. There are,

however, instances where another Perfective Noun
exists as well; among these are the following:

Ziehung	–	Zug
Handlung	–	Handel
Vorsehung	–	Vorsicht
Berufung	–	Beruf
Beziehung	–	Bezug

While the Perfective Nouns in the first group
are semantically very close to what the starred ung-
nominals might have been, had they existed in the
language, the Perfective Nouns such as Zug, Handel,
Vorsicht are semantically much more distant from the ung-
nominals, so that no real overlapping of the two alternating forms of the second group occurs. Although the
Verb ziehen is historically related to Zug, it is doubtful if the speaker of German is actually aware of this
relationship.[5] If this is true, the nouns Zug, Handel,
Beruf, etc. are no longer perceived as the Perfective
Nominal counterpart to the formally related Verbs.[6]
They are rather instances of relexicalizations which
the speaker perceives as separate lexical entries,
whereas the ung-forms fill the slot of the Perfective
Nominals.

We can thus easily specify which Verbs permit an

ung-formation and which do not by introducing a general
convention that would disallow an ung-derivation
wherever there is already a lexically related Perfective
Nominal in the language. I believe that the speaker
of German does exactly that, enabling him to agree
with other speakers about which forms allow the
ung-formation. The ung-suffix becomes an active
word-building element in the language, predictable
from the presence or absence of functionally similar
formatives in the lexicon. This description also
seems to account for the uncertainty of the speaker
of German in some cases as to whether a particular
Verb permits an ung-nominalization or not. There are
certain Verbs, e.g., the group of sein-verbs referred
to above or the Modals, which every speaker will
immediately reject without hesitation. *Könnung,
*Habung, *Bleibung, *Gehung, etc. are clearly
ungrammatical in any speaker's grammar. There are,
however, a number of other forms where native speakers
tend to hesitate at first: e.g., *Beschliessung,
*Steigung, *Begreifung, *Erschreckung, *Verbietung.
In practical tests of these forms I have noticed that
native speakers tend to reject these forms only after
they have found the corresponding grammatical Nominal
forms. This, I feel, is strong evidence for the

plausibility of my description.

One factor frequently pointed out in grammar
books is that ung-derivation is particularly common
in Verbs with prefixes. We get Erholung but not
*Holung, Ausgrabung but not *Grabung, Beratung but not
*Ratung. This curious fact is no accident. For most
prefixes, when attached to a particular Verb, change
the meaning and feature matrix of the Verb to some
extent. It can be determined that modification by
prefixing often makes it possible to describe an
action or event with an end-point in mind, i.e., the
Verbs become ideal candidates for the perfective
ung-nominalization. Consider, e.g., erfahren as
against fahren, überlegen versus legen, verhandeln
versus handeln, entstehen versus stehen, vernehmen
versus nehmen, begeben versus geben and zustellen
versus stellen. While it would be difficult to view
the second of each pair of Verbs with an end-point
in mind, in general the Verbs with the prefixes lend
themselves naturally to such an interpretation.

5.4. Durative Nominal

Before exemplifying the actual treatment of the
ung-nominals in the lexicon, infinitival Nouns (the
other group of Nominals) must be examined. Infinitival

nominalization is a fully productive process in the
language, since virtually every infinitive can be so
nominalized. The result is a Durative Noun that is
syntactically constrained as to gender and number.

There are, of course, infinitival Nouns that
seem somewhat awkward when used in a normal context,
e.g., das Versuchen. But in all these cases it is
not a matter of grammaticalness versus non-grammaticalness
but rather a matter of degree of grammaticalness (or
acceptance). It is obvious that the Noun der Versuch
has begun to take over the function which we expect
das Versuchen to have. It would, however, be unwise
to let the syntax throw out the infinitival Nouns
in those cases where they appear less acceptable.
E.g., in the case of Versuchen there was general
disagreement among native informants whether the form
should be accepted or not; some rejected it entirely,
others felt they would use it in certain environments,
and a third group saw nothing wrong with using it
anywhere. My own intuition is that one can construct
some environment for most infinitive Nouns. If we
contrast das Versuchen, e.g., with another Durative
it sounds quite natural, as may be seen from the
following examples:

(4)   Es handelt sich um das Versuchen und nicht
      um das Gelingen.

The same holds true for other infinitive Nouns. Most
German speakers when asked would reject <u>das Empfangen</u>
in isolation, but in certain environments it, too,
becomes acceptable as in:

(5)   Das Empfangen von Geschenken beleidigt
      ihn nicht.

We shall assume then that the derivation of infinitival
Nominals is a fully productive process. It is clear
that it would not only be undesirable but also
impossible to state syntactic constraints that would
rule out infinitive Nouns in certain environments
as in the following deviant sentences:

(6) *Das Versuchen ist mir misslungen.
(7) *Sein Empfangen des Geschenkes beleidigte
      die anderen.

In fact sentences (6) and (7) seem to be unacceptable
because the context requires, as my analysis would
suggest, a Nominal which is [+ Perfective]. There
seem to be cases, however, where the infinitival
Nominal is almost never allowed. An example of this
kind is <u>das Verloben</u>. Most speakers would never use

this form in their speech. If we look again into
the lexicon for a reason, we note that there are two
Nouns available to the German speaker, Verlöbnis
and Verlobung. Of these two Verlobung is clearly
the Perfective Noun. Verlöbnis, on the other hand,
seems to have taken over much of the function of the
infinitival Verloben. For example, we get sentences
like:

(8) Das Verlöbnis dauerte ein Jahr. (Durative)

(9) Ihre Verlobung haben sie schriftlich
     bekanntgegeben. (Perfective)

Thus again it is the presence of a Durative Noun in
the lexicon which seems to prevent the otherwise
regular process of infinitive nominalization.

5.5. Lexical treatment of Nominals

5.5.1. Semantic conditioning

The reader has, no doubt, noticed that I do not
represent the view of what has been called by some,
autonomous syntax.[7] I firmly believe that a description
of Nominals in German must be concerned with the
semantic conditioning of syntactic rules. My semantic
features [+/- Durative] are an example of such a kind
of conditioning which I shall justify later on

independent syntactic grounds. Another area of concern
that can no longer be ignored is that of lexical
relationships. It may then be possible to show that
many linguistic facts which heretofore could not be
accounted for by means of syntax are the products
of interrelationships of lexical classes. I believe
that Fillmore's case model leads us naturally in a
direction where there will be more concern with
grammatical function--which is really a semantic
concept--than there is in a model that treats a
language purely from a syntactic point of view.

I am not positing something that might be called
a semantic base. However, it seems to me that it will
be much easier to account for cases of semantic
conditioning--the problems of which cannot be overlooked
considering the objections to the Standard Theory
raised by the so-called Generative Semanticists--if
our syntactic base component has been aligned as
closely as possible to functional or semantic
categories, such as the various case categories which
underly our syntactic KP's. In addition, there is
nothing to prevent us from utilizing semantic
features even in syntactic rules of the present
model wherever this leads to a significant linguistic
generalization.

5.5.2. <u>Form</u> <u>of</u> <u>lexical</u> <u>entries</u>

I shall now proceed to illustrate the form of lexical
entries and how our rules would operate to produce
sentences containing the two types of nominalizations
discussed. A set of lexical primes is entered in
the lexicon. Each of these lexical primes may be
interpreted as the underlying form for a particular
group of cognate lexical items. The entry is given
as a two-dimensional matrix in which the columns
represent consecutive segments and the rows represent
any of three types of features: semantic, syntactic,
and phonological. The entries in the matrix of a
particular lexical formative contain only the
idiosyncratic facts, whereas the remaining information
may be derived by universal or language-specific rules.
We shall assume lexical entries to be numbered to
make their reference easier.

Let us now take a particular case, e.g., the group
consisting of the Verb <u>raten</u> and the two Nominal forms
<u>der</u> <u>Rat</u> and <u>das</u> <u>Raten</u>. These cognate forms would be
represented in the lexicon as subentries of the lexical
prime (I):

I   <u>RAT-</u>

$$
\begin{bmatrix}
F_s \text{-----} \\
\cdot \\
\cdot \\
\cdot \\
F_g \text{-----} \\
\cdot \\
\cdot \\
\cdot \\
F_p \text{-----} \\
\cdot \\
\cdot \\
\cdot
\end{bmatrix}
$$

(where F_s = semantic feature, F_g = grammatical feature
(syntactic) and F_p = phonological feature.)

Under this lexical prime there are at least two
subentries ([+Verb] and [+Nominal]):

I.   <u>RAT-</u>

     1.   <u>+VERB</u>:

         <u>RAT-</u>   [+VERB, _____AGT   DAT]

     2.   <u>+NOMINAL</u>:

         1)   <u>RAT-</u>
$\begin{bmatrix} +N, & \begin{bmatrix} -\text{Durative} \\ -\text{ung} \end{bmatrix} & _____\text{AGT} & \text{DAT} \end{bmatrix}$

         2)   <u>RAT-</u>   [+N, [+Durative] _____AGT   DAT]

The first decision a speaker needs to make is whether
he wants to nominalize or use the verbal cognate
instead. If he chooses to nominalize he will select
the rule

NOM ———→ N (KP) ... (KP) Mod

in his grammar at some point. With the NOM-expansion
he also selects an Aspect indicator, either [+Durative]
or [-Durative] in our limited description. A lexical
insertion rule then inserts under the N-node immediately
followed by the Aspect indicator whatever form is
given in the lexicon. In our case, if N + [-Durative]
is introduced, <u>der Rat</u> will be selected. The expansion
N + [+Durative] would result in the lexical form
(I, 2(2)), which is ultimately realized as <u>das Raten</u>.

Now if we suppose that the <u>ung</u>-nominalization
applies to a certain Verb, as in the case of <u>erziehen</u>,
our lexical entry would appear as (II):

II <u>ERZIEH-</u>

1. <u>+VERB</u>:

<u>ERZIEH-</u>   [+VERB, ___AGT   DAT   (I)   ...   ]

2. <u>+NOMINAL</u>:

1) <u>ERZIEH-</u> [+N, [-Durative] ___AGT DAT (I)]

2) <u>ERZIEH-</u> [+N, [+Durative] ___AGT DAT (I)]

In the lexical entry (II, 2(1)) I shall assume
[-Durative] to be equivalent to [-Dur, +ung] since
the [+ung] would be redundant here. I shall only
indicate the absence of the ung-suffix, as in the
case of Rat.

If it turns out that other Perfective Nominal
groups can be isolated out of the -ung-class, it may
be desirable to mark the -ung-types positively. For
it appears that the gender for certain Perfective
Nominals other than the ung-type is predictable as
well. This should be expressed in our description
of German Nominals. Consider the following groups
of Nominals:

> (i)   Flucht, Zucht, Fahrt, Ankunft ...
> (ii) Zug, Flug, Trug, Rat ...

Ignoring the regular consonant alternations such as
g/ch which are needed independently in the language
to take care of such alternations as zog/ziehen
and the also independently required vowel alternations,
we can see that the first group of Perfective Nouns
is apparently composed of stem + t whereas the second
group is made up of the stem alone without a t-suffix.
The first group is made up of Nouns which are
consistently [+Fem] and the second group [+Masc].

I am only indicating some of these subregularities
which, no doubt, need to be explored in the future.

5.5.3. Lexical rules

The lexical entry contains information as to whether
a particular lexical prime has a Perfective ung-nominal
or a Nominal without such an ung-suffix. As was
indicated above, Perfective nominalization entails
a disjunctive process. The speaker searches first
for the Perfective Nominal without ung wherever
possible, and only if none is available does he form
the proper ung-form. This generalization can be made
explicit in form of a lexical rule such as:

$$[-\text{Durative}] \longrightarrow \begin{Bmatrix} [-\text{ung}] \\ [+\text{ung}] \end{Bmatrix}$$

This disjunctively ordered rule states that the
Perfective Nominal without ung is selected first
wherever possible. That is to say, we try the first
expansion consulting the lexicon to see whether such
an expansion would yield a Nominal form. If not,
we try the second expansion deriving the ung-nominal.
If there is no entry in the lexicon for either of the
two expansions, it means that the slot is empty and
no Perfective Nominal is present in the language,

but that there is obviously room for one. That is,
it is a possible but non-existing form.[8] The assumption
that such a Perfective Noun is likely to develop as
time goes on is implicit in this description.

Thus the expansion $[-Dur] \longrightarrow [+ung]$ would
produce the surface form (10):

(10) $_N[ERZIEH]_N$ + $_{Asp}[ung]_{Asp}$.

The expansion $[-Dur] \longrightarrow [-ung]$ would produce the
surface form (11):

(11) $_N[RAT]_N$ + $_{Asp}[\emptyset]_{Asp}$.

The Perfective ung-suffix automatically assigns the
gender feature [+Fem] to the preceding Noun. This
may be accomplished by a general convention, perhaps
applied at the time the ung-suffix is introduced into
the tree. I shall assume at this stage of investigation
that the gender is specified in the lexical entries
for all other Perfective Nouns. If the gender is
found to be predictable for other groups of Perfective
Nouns as well, the gender feature can be introduced
by a general rule in these cases too.

In the case of the infinitival Nouns there will
be a lexical rule $[+Dur] \longrightarrow [en]$ which adjoins

the ending <u>en</u> to the Durative Noun stem in all cases.
This rule produces the surface form (12), for example:

(12) $_N[ERZIEH]_N$ + $_{Asp}[en]_{Asp}$

I shall stipulate that the information [+Dur]/[-Dur]
is preserved throughout the derivational history of a
particular sentence until the brackets are deleted.
This can be done either by preserving it in the Aspect
indicator or by copying it into the Noun itself after
the Aspect marker has been adjoined to it. The
preservation of this information appears desirable since
the +/-Durative distinction is needed to state
certain syntactic constraints, as will be shown in the
following paragraphs.

5.6. Justification of +/-Durative distinction

This analysis of nominalization implies a rejection of
the transformationalist hypothesis--at least for the
types of Nominals treated. I have argued in the
preceding chapter that infinitival Nouns should also
be derived lexically although they do not act like
other lexically introduced Nouns in various respects.
I am now convinced that a transformationalist
treatment of infinitival Nouns in German is not
feasible and that the analysis given here leads to

a more adequate description. Next I shall provide
some further justification for my proposal to reject
the transformational treatment of infinitival Nouns.
At the same time I attempt to justify my base rule
which introduces Aspect into the NOM expansion reading:

$$\text{NOM} \longrightarrow \begin{Bmatrix} \text{NOM} & \text{S} & & & \\ \text{N} & (\text{KP}) & \dots & (\text{KP}) & \text{Mod} \end{Bmatrix}$$

This entails the claim underlying my treatment of
Nominals that the choice of the Aspect feature
determines which one of the two classes of Nominals
discussed in this section is selected.

5.6.1. Determiner argument

I have already shown above that the feature [+/-Durative]
is necessary in order to distinguish between pairs
of Nouns such as Verlöbnis/Verlobung (see sentence (8)
and (9) above). A lexical treatment accounts much
more adequately for the absence of such infinitival
Nominals as das Verloben where there is another Durative
Noun in the lexicon that apparently has taken over
the function of the infinitival Noun.

The feature [+/-Durative] is needed to account
for the following sentences:

(13) Leben ist schön.

(14) Das Leben ist schön.

(15) Schweigen wurde ihm als Strafe auferlegt.

(16) *Das Schweigen wurde ihm als Strafe auferlegt.

(17) Das Schweigen des Waldes war überwältigend.

(18) *Schweigen des Waldes war überwältigend.

Sentence (13) could be translated into English as
'Living is beautiful' and is clearly Durative.
Sentence (14) on the other hand, would be translated
as 'Life is beautiful' with a Perfective interpretation.
Thus the feature [+/-Durative] is needed to account
for the syntactic feature [+/-Det]. The Durative
Nominal Leben cannot take a Determiner in this
enviroment, whereas the Perfective das Leben absolutely
requires it.[9] The restrictions in the use of Determiner
with the Durative Nominal in contrast to the Perfective
interpretation requires a N + Aspect analysis. Note
that Schweigen also has both a Perfective and a Durative
interpretation. It would, therefore, have two entries
in the lexicon. This double nature of Schweigen can
also be demonstrated by substituting for Schweigen
another Perfective Noun--namely Stille--which has a
similar range of meaning:

(19) Die Stille des Waldes war überwältigend.

(20) *Die Stille wurde ihm als Strafe auferlegt.

(21) *Stille wurde ihm als Strafe auferlegt.

Whenever <u>Schweigen</u> is a Perfective Noun it may be
replaced by <u>Stille</u> as in sentence (19). But whenever
<u>Schweigen</u> is a Durative it cannot be replaced by <u>Stille</u>,
as in sentences (20) and (21).

5.6.2. <u>Adjectival</u> <u>modifier</u> <u>argument</u>

If the above Nouns are modified by an Adjective similar
results are obtained. Consider the sentences:

(22) Frommes Leben war sein Ziel.

(23) *Das fromme Leben war sein Ziel.

(24) Das gute Leben in Amerika hat ein Ende.

(25) *Gutes Leben in Amerika hat ein Ende.

Sentence (23) is not possible with a Durative interpretation that could be rendered in English as 'Pious living
was his goal'. Sentence (24) would have to be translated
as 'The good life in America is all over'. This
Perfective interpretation is not possible for sentence
(25), however.

5.6.3. Relativization argument

The next argument concerns relativization, as in the
following sentences:

(26) *Leben, das er führt, ist schön.

(27) *Leben, das der Mensch von Gott empfängt,
      ist schön.

(28) Das Leben, das er führt, ist schön.

(29) Das Leben, das der Mensch von Gott empfängt,
      ist schön.

Both the restrictive relative clause (26) and the
non-restrictive relative clause (27) are impossible
with the Durative interpretation. The Perfective
Leben, however, can take both restrictive and
non-restrictive clauses freely.

Thus it has been shown that, for syntactic reasons,
it is desirable to have the [+/-Durative] marker in
the NOM expansion in order to be able to state syntactic
constraints which would otherwise be difficult to
state. At the same time it is apparent that a
transformational derivation of the two sentences (13)
and (14)

(13) Leben ist schön.

(14) Das Leben ist schön.

from an underlying deep structure (T13-14) would be
problematic in any grammar:

(T13-14)

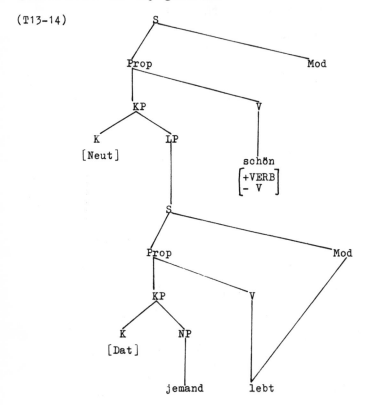

5.6.4. <u>Extraposition argument</u>

The next argument concerns extraposition. Nouns like
<u>das Essen</u>, <u>das Wissen</u>, <u>das Denken</u> have to be interpreted
as either [+Dur], translated into English as 'eating',
'knowing' and 'thinking' respectively, or as [-Dur]
in which case it would be rendered into English as
'the food', 'the knowledge' and 'the way of thinking'

respectively. Consider now the following sentences:

(30) Essen its ungesund.

(31) Das Essen ist ungesund.

(32) Leben ist schön.

(33) Das Leben ist schön.

If we apply extraposition to these sentences the result
would be:

(34) Es ist ungesund zu essen.

(35) *Es ist ungesund das Essen.

(36) Es ist schön zu leben.

(37) *Es ist schön das Leben.

Extraposition is not possible in cases where a **Perfective**
Nominal occurs. Sentences (35) and (37) could perhaps
be used in poetry, but not in non-affective every-day
speech. Even then the <u>es</u> is not the extraposed
empty <u>es</u>, but rather a pronominal anticipation of
<u>das Essen</u> or <u>das Leben</u>. Only the Durative forms can
undergo the extraposition transformation without
becoming ungrammatical.

5.6.5. <u>More</u> <u>observations</u> <u>about</u> <u>Determiners</u>

The presence versus absence of the Determiner for
such nouns as <u>Essen/das Essen</u>, <u>Leben/das Leben</u>,

<u>Schweigen/das Schweigen</u>, <u>Treffen/das Treffen</u>,
<u>Denken/das Denken</u>, <u>Wissen/das Wissen</u> can be explained
with the feature opposition [+/-Durative]. However,
there are other cases of [+/-Determiner] contrast
which can have nothing to do with the [+/-Dur] opposition
Consider the following sentences where only a [+Durative]
interpretation of the Nouns in question is possible:

    (38)   Das Gehen strengt an.

    (39)   Gehen strengt an.

    (40)   Schlafen ist die schönste Beschäftigung,
         die es gibt.

    (41)   Das Schlafen ist die schönste Beschäftigung,
         die es gibt.

    (42)   Reisen macht Spass.

    (43)   Das Reisen macht Spass.

When questioned most speakers agreed that there is a
slight difference between the two sentences of the
three pairs above differing only in the presence or
absence of an Article in the surface structure. When
asked what the difference might be--although there
was no complete agreement among my informants--the
majority indicated that the sentence with the definite
Article should be interpreted slightly more specific
in some way, whereas the one without the Article

appeared to have a more generic, unspecific
interpretation. Some even wanted to include a specific
referent, indicating that they preferred a sentence
like (38') to sentence (38) above:

(38') Das Gehen strengt ihn an.

It does not matter, apparently, as in the case of
sentence (43), whether the specific referent is of the
form (44a) or (44b):

(44a) Das Reisen macht ihm Spass.

(44b) Das Reisen mit dem Zug macht Spass.

Before we try to interpret the above data, we need to
look at another group of examples. Everyone of the
infinitive Nouns in sentences (38) - (43) belongs to
what has traditionally been called <u>intransitives</u>.

If we turn to those forms which fall under the
traditional category <u>transitives</u> we get a very similar
picture:

(45) Anziehen dauert lange.

(46) Das Anziehen dauert lange.

(47) Rauchen verursacht Krebs.

(48) Das Rauchen verursacht Krebs.

The same alternation of [+/-Determiner] occurs with the

transitive forms, cf. (45) versus (46) and (47) versus
(48). For native speakers there is again a difference
in meaning. It appears that sentences (45) and (47)
must be interpreted just like the intransitives (39)
and (42). Sentences (46) and (48), on the other hand,
seem to have an implicit reference to the Object
of the action, thereby linking it to a specific event.
Thus sentence (46) should probably be rendered as
(46') and (48) as (48'):

> (46') Das Anziehen (von etwas) dauert lange.
>
> (48') Das Rauchen (von Zigaretten) verursacht
>   Krebs.

The Article implies here a specific reference, which
shows up as an adjunct to the infinitive NP, in our
case realized as a surface Genitive. It does not
matter whether this adjunct derives from an underlying
Neutral, as in (49), or from a Dative as in (50), or
perhaps from some other element:

> (49) Das Anziehen des Mantels dauert lange.
>
> (50) Das Anziehen der Kinder dauert lange.

It seems then that in the transitive as well as in the
intransitive cases the sentences containing a definite
Article make reference to a specific event which may

either be determined by the larger context of the
discourse (as in <u>das Anziehen der Kinder</u>) or be
implicit in the infinitive Noun itself (as in
<u>das Anziehen der Kleider</u>). In order to account for
the definite Article in the one case but not in the
other, I propose the following deep structures (T45)
and (T46) for sentences (45) and (46) respectively:

(T45)

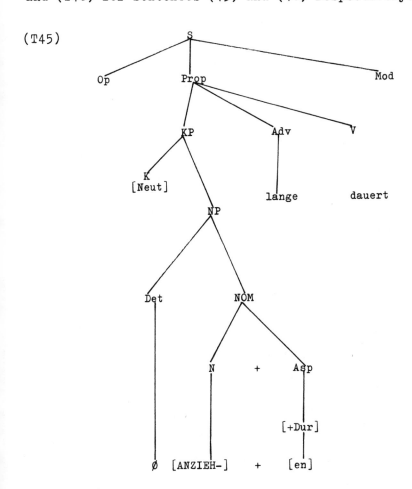

(T46)

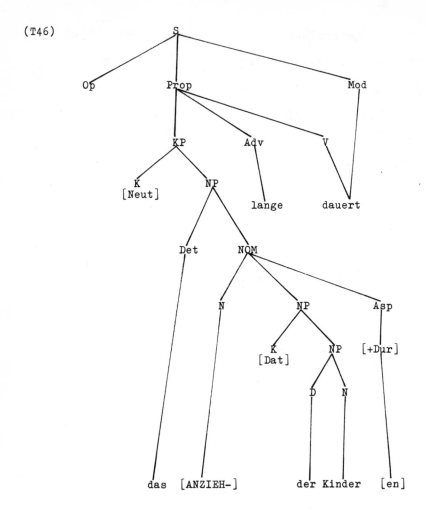

This analysis indicates that what occurs under the
NOM node determines the presence or absence of the
Article. If N + Mod are the only elements under NOM
no article will show up in the surface structure under
the Det node. However, if there are any other elements
under NOM--usually KP's--then the definite Article will

be generated. This may be done by a transformation
that assigns the feature [+Specific] to the Determiner
element preceding the Nominal in cases where there
is at least one additional KP selected in the NOM
expansion. Interpreted this means that the reference
to a specific event--reflected in the presence of an
additional KP under NOM--triggers the attachment of
the feature [+Specific] under the Det node of the
head of the NOM expansion.

I am not concerned at this point with the treatment
of the temporal Adverb <u>lange</u> and have introduced the
adverbial node only for simplification.

My treatment of sentences (45) and (46) entails
the claim that, whenever the Article occurs in the
surface form, a deep structure of the type (T46) with
an expansion NOM ⟶ [N + KP ... Mod] may be expected.
The KP can sometimes be optionally deleted. Whenever
there is no Article in the surface structure I shall
assume the deep structure of the type (T45) with an
expansion NOM ⟶ [N ∅ Mod].

This analysis is supported by independent syntactic
evidence of the following examples:

(51)   Das Kommen der Tante führt immer zu Zwistigkeiten.

(52)   *Kommen der Tante führt immer zu Zwistigkeiten.

(53)   Das Geben von Geschenken bringt Segen.

(54)   *Geben von Geschenken bringt Segen.

(55)   Das Anziehen der Kinder dauert lange.

(56)   *Anziehen der Kinder dauert lange.

For these sentences the deep structure (T46) must be
assumed, i.e., the NOM expansion is of the form:

NOM $\longrightarrow$ [N   KP   ...   Mod].

According to my analysis there should then be a definite
Article in the surface structure in all these cases,
which is exactly what is found. This explains why
sentences (52), (54), and (56) are ungrammatical, whereas
sentences (45) and (47) are grammatical.

My analysis also accounts for the well-known
restrictions on relativization, as may be seen from
the following sentences:

(57)   Das Rauchen, das ich mir nicht abgewöhnen
       kann, ist schädlich.

(58)   *Rauchen, das ich mir nicht abgewöhnen kann,
       ist schädlich.

The definite Article is again required in the case of
relativization. As one might expect, sentence (58) is
ungrammatical. The analysis can easily be extended
to the examples that contain relative clauses. For
as was stated above, if the NOM expansion includes
an element other than [N + Mod] the definite Article
insertion applies. Thus, what seemed intuitively to
be the right analysis is supported by independent
syntactic evidence.

5.7.   Concluding remarks

A few words are necessary to justify my NOM node.
Initially I felt that no intervening NOM node was
necessary. However, as mentioned in chapter 4, this
node is needed to express generalizations that would
otherwise be difficult to capture. The NOM node is
necessary in order to describe the environment for
the definite Article insertion with [+Durative]
Nominals. It is also necessary for the introduction
of the Aspect marker which is essential for my analysis
of Perfective and Durative Nominals. I believe,
therefore, that there must be an intervening NOM
node in the tree.

It is assumed here that my generalizations about
these two classes of Nominals have correlates within

the competence of the speaker-hearer and represent,
therefore, true generalizations about the grammatical
processes of German. My analysis has ignored other
types of derived Nouns in German which must be left
for further investigation. It may be possible to fit
into the category [+/-Durative] other Nominal types,
such as the Nouns formed from Verbs with the suffix
<u>nis</u>. <u>Nis</u>-nominals appear to be for the most part
Perfective Nouns.[10]

It may in the future perhaps be necessary to define
and add another Aspect category or even modify the
present categories. This can easily be accomplished
within the framework which has been provided in this
section.

It has thus been shown that both types of
nominalizations, the Perfective <u>ung</u>-nouns and the
infinitival Nouns are best derived lexically rather
than transformationally from an underlying sentence.
By introducing an Aspect indicator into the base rules,
I have been able to predict which type of Nominal
must be introduced into the tree. In addition, this
treatment has allowed me to show that both the <u>ung</u>
and the infinitival nominalizations are regular and
active processes in the language. The extent to which
these nominalization processes are regular depends

on the interrelationship of lexical formatives so
that, in general, one lexical item is sufficient to
fill a particular slot in the language to avoid the
existence of what might be called <u>homolexons</u>: two
or more lexical items for any one particular function.

Thus the regularity of these nominalization
processes demonstrates some features of the systematic
interrelationships among members of the lexicon.
It seems to be the nature of these interreslationships
(1) to establish certain corresponding lexical slots
in different lexical classes, (2) to fill each existing
slot by providing a distinct lexical form for it,
and (3) to prevent the occurrence of 'homolexons',
i.e., two or more lexical items for any particular
function.

6. THE ROLE OF LEXICAL HEAD NOUNS IN COMPLEMENTATION

6.1. NP or VP-complementation

In the next two sections I shall be concerned
with complementation in German. The first question
to be considered is whether we are dealing with
NP-complementation or VP-complementation. Perhaps
even both types have to be assumed. NP-complements
may simply be defined as structures where a complement
is always dominated by an NP node. VP-complements--if
they exist--do not require such an intervening NP
node, but may be directly attached to the VP of the
sentence. A generally held opinion is that there are
probably no cases of VP-complementation in English,
as had earlier been suggested by Rosenbaum (1967).
This is the view which the authors of the UESP
grammar (1968:538ff.) express. We need not review
the arguments advanced for English, since these are

irrelevant in determining the status of complements
in German.

In order to determine whether German can be
described in terms of NP-complementation alone, I
constructed a questionnaire using the tests to
distinguish NP-complementation from VP-complementation
that have been employed for English: cleft, pseudo
cleft, interrogative test and extra-position test.

The following represents a sample of the 70
sentences contained in the questionnaire:

(1) Der Mann weiss, dass er zu Hause ist.

(2) Was der Mann weiss, ist, dass er zu Hause ist.

(3) Es ist, dass er zu Hause ist, was der Mann weiss.

(4) Ist es, dass er zu Hause ist, was der Mann weiss?

(5) Es ist die Tatsache, dass er zu Hause ist,
     was der Mann weiss.

The sentences (2) - (5) above all sound very
unnatural, though perhaps not entirely ungrammatical.
The response to the questionnaire demonstrated that
it is difficult for the native speaker to decide
whether these sentences are grammatical. Respondents
to the questionnaire were to mark each sentence as
belonging to one of three categories: grammatical,
ungrammatical, and undecided. The responses for all but

the first two sentences were evenly divided among
the three groups. This inconsistency was characteristic
of the answers to the questionnaire as a whole, thus
indicating that the tests are of little use for
deciding between NP-complementation and VP-complementation
in German. Since the clause <u>dass er zu Hause ist</u> is
obviously an NP under the Objective node, and the
sentence formed by applying the various tests sound
very unnatural and do not yield consistent results,
I had to abandon them altogether.[1]

I shall assume here that all cases of complementation treated in this section represent some kind of
NP-complementation. If VP-complementation is also
required, it can easily be introduced later. Up to
this point I have not found any cases that require
such treatment in order to provide for descriptive
or explanatory adequacy.

6.2. <u>Lexical</u> <u>head</u> <u>Nouns</u> <u>in</u> <u>complements</u>

Assuming then that we are basically dealing with cases
of NP-complementation, we have to determine whether
the internal structure of the NP dominating complements
corresponds to Fig (1a) or (1b):

(a)   (b)

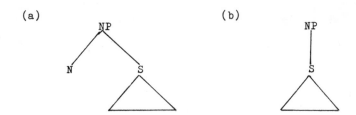

Fig (1):   Structure of NP-complements

That is, does the complement represent the only element
dominated by NP, as in Fig (1b), or is there an
additional lexical head Noun present as in (1a).

There is clear evidence for cases of lexical
head Nouns in English. The Kiparskys (1968) have
given a number of persuasive arguments for the
existence of the lexical head Noun <u>fact</u> in the deep
structure with certain Verbs and Adjectives which they
call Factives. Although there are problems with some
of the syntactic arguments given by the Kiparskys,
the status of <u>fact</u> as a lexical head Noun in deep
structures containing Factive Verbs and Adjectives
has been generally accepted for English.[2]

A similar attempt to justify other lexical head
Nouns such as <u>notion</u>, <u>idea</u>, <u>action</u>, etc. has been
made by Peter Menzel (1969). Although the introduction
of additional head Nouns has enabled him to show some
additional syntactic regularities, the arguments for
the head Nouns posited by Menzel are much less

convincing as those for the Noun <u>fact</u>.[3]

Since the Kiparskys (1968:15ff.) have suggested
that the distinction [+/-Factive] also holds for other
languages, including German, I shall now turn to German
to see if the evidence supports this claim.

6.2.1. <u>DIE</u> <u>TATSACHE</u> as <u>lexical</u> <u>head</u> <u>Noun</u>

The German equivalent to <u>fact</u>, <u>die Tatsache</u>, is less
common on the surface and, if it is introduced into a
sentence, it sounds far less natural than the form
without <u>Tatsache</u>. There are cases, however, where
<u>die Tatsache</u> does precede the <u>dass</u>-clause in the surface
form as in:

(6) Die Tatsache, dass er spät nach Hause kam,
     erregte meine Mutter.

Thus it cannot be ruled out as ungrammatical with
certain Verbs and Adjectives. Consider a few examples
of this type:

(7) Die Tatsache, dass er entlassen wurde, ist
     ärgerlich.

(8) Die Tatsache, dass sie verloren haben, ist
     ausschlaggebend.

(9) Die Tatsache, dass es keine Spuren gibt,
     ist bedeutsam.

(10) *Die Tatsache, dass der Hund bellt, ist
     wahrscheinlich.

(11) *Die Tatsache, dass er gestorben ist, ist wahr.

(12) *Die Tatsache, dass er entlassen wird, ist
     falsch.

Sentences (7) - (9) permit the Noun <u>die Tatsache</u> in the
surface form although these sentences perhaps do not
sound as natural as the corresponding forms without
<u>die Tatsache</u>, but this seems to depend on the structure
of the rest of the sentence rather than on anything
inherent in the Adjective or Verb. Consider, e.g.:

(13) Die Tatsache, dass er sich dabei das Bein
      gebrochen hat, ist wirklich ärgerlich.

(14) Die amtlich berichtete Tatsache, dass die
      Hinrichtung gestern stattgefunden hat,
      ist tragisch.

Sentence (13) sounds much more natural than sentence (8).
In sentence (14) there is additional indication that
<u>die Tatsache</u> has to be in the deep structure, since it
can occur on the surface with one or more modifiers.
In this case the Noun <u>Tatsache</u> itself cannot be deleted.

6.2.2. Arguments for Factive/Nonfactive

6.2.2.1. DASS-complement argument

The validity of the [+/-Factive] distinction among
German Adjectives can be established by determining
whether die Tatsache is permitted with a dass-complement
or not. The following two lists give some examples
of Factive and Nonfactive Adjectives:

Factive	Nonfactive
bedeutsam	wahr
traurig	schlecht
erwähnenswert	wahrscheinlich
ärgerlich	möglich
wichtig	sicher
beweiskräftig	schön
tragisch	gewiss

The same distinction can be established for Verbs as
well. Consider the following sentences:

(15) Die Tatsache, dass sie sich auf den Ellbogen
     stützte, regte ihn auf.

(16) Die Tatsache, dass die Wahlen vor der Tür
     stehen, genügt, um ihn milde zu stimmen.

(17) Die Tatsache, dass wir zu Hause sind,
       bedeutet nicht, dass wir auch Besuch
       empfangen.

(18) *Die Tatsache, dass er spielt, kommt vor.

(19) *Die Tatsache, dass er sich die Haare
       schneiden lässt, scheint mir.

(20) *Die Tatsache, dass das Auto stehen bleibt,
       passiert.

Sentences (15) - (20) are examples of Verbs which take
dass-clauses as Subject. Of these only the Verbs in
(15) - (17) allow the head Noun die Tatsache to precede
the dass-complement and are, therefore, Factives.
The Verbs in sentences (18) - (20), on the other
hand, do not permit the noun die Tatsache, i.e., they
are Nonfactives.

Notice again that although not every German
speaker may be entirely happy with the sound of
sentence (15), hardly anyone will object to this
sentence if the environment is slightly modified to
(21):

(21) Die unbedeutende Tatsache, dass sie sich
       beim Essen auf den Ellbogen stützte,
       regte ihn dermassen auf.

Among the Factive and Nonfactive Verbs are those in
the following lists:

Factive	Nonfactive
bedeuten	vorkommen
erregen	scheinen
bereuen	behaupten
übersehen	glauben
beweisen	wissen
überzeugen	sich vormachen
anregen	aussehen
erfahren	passieren
entscheiden	beschliessen
	ausdenken

The preceding lists of Verbs include both those
that take a <u>dass</u>-clause as surface Subject and those
that take it as surface Object. The following
examples show that the same division holds for those
Verbs that take the <u>dass</u>-clause as Object:

(22) Er bereut die Tatsache, dass er das Auto
zu spät zum Stehen gebracht hat.

(23) Er regt sich über die lächerliche Tatsache
auf, dass seine Wirtin die Eier vor dem
Servieren immer ableckt.

(24) *Er glaubt die Tatsache, dass es draussen
     regnet.

(25) *Er weiss die Tatsache, dass der Strauss
     einen Schnurrbart trägt.

There is then a clear distinction between Verbs and
Adjectives which allow the Noun <u>die Tatsache</u> on the
surface with a following <u>dass</u>-complement and others
which never do.

6.2.2.2. <u>Nominalization</u> <u>argument</u>

A division exists also with regard to other constructions.
E.g., <u>die Tatsache</u> is realized as a surface Genitive
when the following complement has been nominalized,
as in the following sentences:

(26) Die Tatsache seines unmöglichen Benehmens
     stimmte die Mutter traurig.

(27) Die Tatsache seines ewigen Unterbrechens
     geht mir allmählich auf die Nerven.

(28) Er bereut die Tatsache seines Ehebruchs
     nicht.

(29) *Die Tatsache seines Unfalls scheint mir.

(30) *Er glaubt die Tatsache seines grossen Verlusts.

(31) *Meine Frau erdenkt sich die Tatsache ihres
     Kochens.

6.2.2.3. <u>Semantic</u> <u>argument</u>

The Kiparskys have also shown that a semantic difference,
that gives the <u>dass</u>-clauses with Factive Verbs a
force lacking in <u>dass</u>-clauses with Nonfactive Verbs,
is correlated with the syntactic difference. In
Factive sentences 'the speaker presupposes that the
embedded clause expresses a true proposition, and makes
some assertion about that proposition. All predicates
which behave syntactically as factives have this
semantic property, and almost none of those which
behave syntactically as non-factives have it'
(Kiparskys 1968:7). They go on to suggest that one
distinguish the following three things:

'(1)   What the speaker presupposes to be true

(2)   What the speaker believes to be true

(3)   What the speaker asserts to be true'

and claim that 'factivity depends on presupposition,
and not on belief or assertion' (7). This distinction
is--as one would expect--also true for German in the
same way. Consider the sentences:

(32)   Ich glaube, dass Karl nicht zu Hause ist.
       (Nonfactive)

(33)   Dass Karl nicht zu Hause ist, bedeutet nichts.
       (Factive)

Only in sentence (33) does the speaker presuppose that
the proposition <u>Karl ist nicht zu Hause</u> is true.   In
sentence (32), on the other hand, the same proposition
is only believed to be true.

6.2.2.4. <u>Subjunctive</u> <u>argument</u>

The Kiparskys have suggested that the Factive/Nonfactive
distinction may also play a role in explaining the
subjunctive rule, since, as they observe correctly, the
'subordinate clauses in German are not in the subjunctive
mood if the truth of the clause is presupposed by the
speaker' (15-16).   They propose that the subjunctive
rule is 'inapplicable in factives and optional in
nonfactives' (16).   The following two examples are
taken from their paper:

(34)   Er behauptet, dass die Erde flach sei (ist).

(35)   Er versteht, dass die Erde rund ist (*sei).

But notice now sentence (36)

(36)   Er versteht, dass die Erde rund sein soll (solle).

where with <u>verstehen</u> the subjunctive is possible, if we
introduce the Modal <u>sollen</u> into the <u>dass</u>-clause.

Now let us consider the following Nonfactives:

(37)   Es ist möglich, dass er zu Hause ist.

(38)   *Es ist möglich, dass er zu Hause sei.

(39)   Es ist wahrscheinlich, dass die Erde rund ist.

(40)   *Es ist wahrscheinlich, dass die Erde rund sei.

(41)   Ich glaube, dass der Mann krank ist.

(42)   *Ich glaube, dass der Mann krank sei.

Sentence (36) is a problem if the Modal is introduced into
the deep structure, which would then look something
like (43):

(43)   Er versteht $_{NP}$[dass die Erde rund sein solle]$_{NP}$

But if the embedding analysis of subjective Modals is
chosen, which we have briefly referred to in chapter 2,
an explanation is possible. The deep structure for
(36) under this proposal would look like (44):

(44)   Er versteht $_S$[dass es sein soll

       $_{NP}$[dass die Erde rund ist (sei)]$_{NP}$]$_S$

This analysis would mean that the dass-complement
[dass die Erde rund ist] is not embedded under the
Neutral node which is part of the expansion that
generates the Factive Verb verstehen, but under the
Neutral node that is part of the expansion generating
the Nonfactive Modal SOLLEN. That would explain why

string (36) is grammatical, if the subjunctive rule
has applied, while string (35) is not.

This, however, does not yet account for why
sentences (37) - (42) do not permit the subjunctive
rule, although they are Nonfactives, i.e., the proposition
expressed in the dass-clause is not presupposed to be
true by the speaker. If the distinction Factive/Nonfactive
is at all relevant in deciding when the subjunctive
rule applies, it should certainly be applicable in
these instances. The above sentences can be explained,
however, if the subdivision among Nonfactives, already
given by the Kiparskys, is taken into account. They
divided this group into two categories, namely:

(1) What the speaker believes to be true
(2) What the speaker asserts to be true.

All of the above exceptions fall into category (1);
i.e., whenever the dass-clause contains 'what the
speaker believes to be true' no subjunctive is possible.
But whenever the dass-clause contains 'what the speaker
asserts to be true' the subjunctive becomes possible
as in:

(45) Die Frau erklärt ihrem Sohn, dass der Schnee
weiss ist (sei).

If this analysis were correct, the distinction
would not be between Factives and Nonfactives but
rather between Factives and the first category of the
Nonfactives as against the second category of the
Nonfactives.

But if more evidence is being considered it becomes
clear that this distinction doesn't suffice to account
for the occurrence of the subjunctive in dass-clauses.
Whatever the factors involved are, they must be much
more complex. Consider, e.g., the sentences:

(46) Er sagte, dass sein Vater nicht zu Hause
      ist (sei).

(47) Er behauptet, dass sie nicht kommt (komme).

(48) Er glaubte, dass sie ihn nun endgültig aus
      dem Haus geschmissen haben (hätten).

(49) Er nimmt an, dass ich das Buch nicht gelesen
      habe (hätte).

(50) Er wünschte, dass er Millionär (*ist) wäre.

(51) Er wünscht, dass man ihn endlich in Ruhe liesse.

(52) Der Bauer befahl dem Knecht, dass er den
      Kuhstall ausmisten sollte.

(53) Die Mutter sagt, dass die Kinder nicht immer
      auf die Bäume klettern sollten.

The subjunctive rule in German appears to be a

case of semantic conditioning of a syntactic transformation.

As long as the semantic condition can be identified
with a clearly definable group or groups of lexical
items, it can easily be incorporated into our model
of description.[4] However, I am convinced that the
semantic feature [+/-Factive] proposed by the Kiparskys
is not the answer to the problem of subjunctive in
German. As I will show below, it is just not true
that the insertion of subjunctive is an optional rule,
as the Kiparskys (1968:16) have suggested. It is
clearly semantically distinct from the corresponding
indicative form.

Judging from sentences (46) - (53) above, it
seems that there are four properties of Matrix Verbs
that are relevant for the operation of the subjunctive
rule: [+Assertion], [+Wish], [-Belief], [+Command].
Whenever a Matrix Verb is marked negative for the
feature [Belief] or positive for any of the other
three features it permits the optional application of
the subjunctive rule to its dass-complement. I am
including doubt under the feature [-Belief], so that
bezweifeln would have [-Belief] among its feature
entries. These features would then suffice to account
for the subjunctive in sentences (46) - (53). The

Verbs in sentences (46), (47), and (53) are marked
[+Assertion], the Verbs in (48) and (49) [-Belief],
(50) and (51) [+Wish], and (52) [+Command].

This analysis would account for the fact that
dass-complements of Factive Verbs do not permit the
subjunctive rule to apply, as is demonstrated by
sentences (54) and (55):

(54)   Nixon bereut, dass er kein Demokrat ist (*sei).

(55)   Der Fahrer erkennt, dass das Auto langsam aber
       sicher auf ihn zukommt (*zukomme).

It also predicts that the subjunctive would be
ungrammatical in dass-complements of Nonfactives such
as the following:

(56)   Es ist möglich, dass das Auto sofort anspringt
       (*anspringe).

(57)   Es ist wahr, dass die Gedanken frei sind (*seien).

(58)   Es ist ärgerlich, dass alles so teuer wird
       (*werde).

In other words the Factive/Nonfactive distinction is not
relevant here at all; it makes possible only one
sub-generalization: Factives--among others--do not take
the subjunctive in their complements.

The subjunctive could be introduced into the

<u>dass</u>-complement transformationally. It would then,
however, be necessary to stipulate that the information
[+Assertion], [+Wish], [-Belief], [+Command] is
preserved-perhaps as a feature under the Verb-until the
subjunctive insertion applies. But there are problems
with this procedure as well. The most basic objection
to this approach is that the subjunctive transformation
would have to be optional, i.e., a stylistic,
non-semantic variation only. All German speakers,
however, would agree that utterance (59) differs from
(60) or (61) differs from (62):

> (59)   Er glaubte, dass seine Frau kein Geld hat.
>
> (60)   Er glaubte, dass seine Frau kein Geld habe.
>
> (61)   Sie sagte zu mir, dass sie nicht kommt.
>
> (62)   Sie sagte zu mir, dass sie nicht komme.

It is apparent that the subjunctive rule is not just a
stylistic change but that there is a semantic distinction
as well, no matter how slight it may be. Sentence (62)
may for many speakers contain the presupposition:
<u>she is coming after all</u>, i.e., she was lying to me,
but sentence (61) could not normally be interpreted
this way.

One thing is clear, that there are semantic facts
which determine the application of the subjunctive rule.

I cannot see how a purely syntactic treatment could
account for the facts at hand. It will, therefore,
be necessary to utilize semantic features to trigger
the introduction of the subjunctive. Within the
framework that has been provided here, this could be
done in the operator.

The set of semantic properties that requires the
subjunctive will have to be determined by considering
all the uses of subjunctive in German, which is
extremely complex. It should, however, be possible
to integrate the treatment of the subjunctive so as
to include also the subjunctive forms of subjective
Modals. The subjective Modals can be lined up
easily on a scale of certainty--designated by a
sequence of integers--ranging approximately from
müssen as the Modal which expresses the greatest
degree of certainty to mögen which conveys the least
degree of certainty. Every Modal can be considered
to represent one state along this certainty scale.
Each state in turn can be divided into a plus and a
minus state, where the plus state is represented by
the indicative form of a particular Modal and the
minus state by the subjunctive. Thus whenever the
speaker chooses the minus state of some feature F_i,
[Certainty], the subjunctive rule applies. It seems

to me that this same feature [+/-Certainty] may be
sufficient also to account for the other occurrences
of subjunctive, e.g., with the various complementizers.

I suggest, therefore, that underlying the use of
subjunctive both with subjective Modals and otherwise
is only one feature, which I will call [-Certainty].
Whether the feature [+/-Certainty] represents a binary
distinction referring to one state along a scale of
certainty or not is irrelevant. How this uncertainty
is interpreted or utilized in social context depends
to a large degree on other factors such as discourse,
social customs, and other basically cognitive elements;
e.g., whether the speaker says (63) or (64)

(63) Könnte ich noch eine Tasse Kaffee haben?

(64) Kann ich noch eine Tasse Kaffee haben?

is usually interpreted as a matter of politeness. But
the real reason why sentence (63) is perceived as more
polite is that the speaker appears less sure of
himself and seems to leave the decision to the listener.
He imparts a much greater sense of uncertainty whether
he will actually receive the cup of coffee or not.

It seems to me that the description of the subjective
use of Modals and the subjunctive _must_ and _can_ go hand
in hand. The subjective Modals can be introduced on a

scale of certainty of which each feature F_i, [Certainty],
has two states + and -, which are realized as indicative
or subjunctive respectively. The indicative/subjunctive
alternation apart from the subjective Modals, as in
indirect discourse, in wish, or polite requests,
is made dependent on the same [+/-Certainty] distinction
in the operator, except that no scalar values need
be assigned to the certainty feature apart from the
Modals.

If this analysis of subjunctive is correct, we
have a simple and uniform way of introducing the
subjunctive into the tree when needed. This description,
which relies basically on semantic conditioning of
the syntactic subjunctive rule, also expresses adequately
the semantic distinction the speaker of German perceives.
By leaving out the cognitive implications (doubt,
politeness, lying, etc.), we account at the same time
for the fact that no two native speakers of German
exactly agree on the semantic distinction between two
sentences which differ only in respect to the indicative
or subjunctive form of the Verb.

6.2.2.5. Pronominalization argument

The Kiparskys pointed out another syntactic phenomenon:
the occurrence of the pronoun it optionally before

that-clauses with Factive Verbs. The very same
phenomenon is found in German. The interpretation of
it as a reduced form of the fact seems very attractive,
allowing one to account for the presence of this proform
in a simple way.

The following sentences with Factive Verbs permit
an optional es before the dass-complement:

(65) Der Mann bereut es, dass er nach Berlin
      gefahren ist.

(66) Der Mann bereut, dass er nach Berlin
      gefahren ist.

(67) Das Mädchen versteht es nicht, dass sie
      ihren Vater nicht sehen darf.

(68) Das Mädchen versteht nicht, dass sie ihren
      Vater nicht sehen darf.

(69) *Der Junge glaubt es, dass er die Schule
      schwänzen kann.

(70) *Ich weiss es, dass der Regenbogen mehrfarbig
      ist.

(71) *Der Fahrer behauptet es, dass er den Wagen
      nicht gesehen hat.

There is a difference between this es, which must
be considered a proform of the lexical head of the
complement, whether this lexical head Noun is

die <u>Tatsache</u> or perhaps some other Noun, and the
expletive <u>es</u>. Consider, therefore, a few examples
containing the expletive <u>es</u>. Sentence (72)

(72) Es ist möglich, dass er zu Hause ist.

can also be changed into

(72') Dass er zu Hause ist, ist möglich.

just as sentence (73)

(73) Es ist wahrscheinlich, dass ich ihn nicht
      mehr sehen werde.

can be changed into

(73') Dass ich ihn nicht mehr sehen werde, ist
      wahrscheinlich.

The semantic difference between the <u>es</u> in sentence (65),
e.g., and the <u>es</u> in (72) was also noted by the Kiparskys
for English. This difference may be demonstrated with
a Verb such as <u>erwarten</u> which is ambiguous with regard
to factivity. The sentence

(74) Ich habe erwartet, dass er zum Essen da ist.

may be continued with (<u>Aber der Zug hat wohl Verspätung</u>)
But sentence (75)

(75) Ich habe es erwartet, dass er zum Essen da ist.

could only be continued with a statement such as
(<u>Sonst kommt er nie, aber wenn es was zu essen gibt</u>,
<u>dann lässt er sich sehen</u>).

Notice that the introduction of the Factive <u>es</u>
in (75) changes the meaning of sentence (74)
considerably. The proposition in the <u>dass</u>-clause of
(75) is presupposed to be true by the speaker; in
sentence (74) the implication is that the proposition
is not true.[5]

6.2.2.6. <u>Concluding</u> <u>remarks</u>

Having seen then that the Factive/Nonfactive distinction
is needed for syntactic and semantic explanatory
reasons-whether this is actually the correctly formulated
feature or not-let us consider what implications the
introduction of a lexical head Noun would have for our
base rules. The Kiparskys suggest that Factive and Nonfactive complements have deep structures which differ
in the following way:

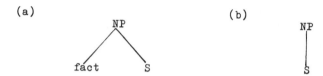

(a)   (b)

Fig (2): DS configuration for Factive/Nonfactive
          complements

This analysis has been largely accepted in treatments of nominalization and has been incorporated into my base rule which expands LP as

$$LP \longrightarrow (L) \quad S$$

where the optional lexical head may be realized among others as die Tatsache if it occurs under the Objective node of an expansion which generates a Factive Verb.

There are, of course, other lexical head Nouns which can occur under the Neutral node, e.g., der Glaube in the following sentence taken from Schulz-Griesbach (1964:268):

(76) Der Glaube, dass wir in Gottes Hand sind,
     kann Berge versetzen.

Although the lexical head Noun die Tatsache is less common in German--at least on the surface--I will show below that the notion lexical head is extremely important in a total account of German complementation, since it will enable us to account for Hartung's Quasi-Nominalisierungen (1964:62ff.) in a simple manner not possible otherwise.

6.3. Treatment of Demonstrative particles

6.3.1. Hartung's proposal

In order to see the simplicity of my own proposal more clearly, it will be necessary to look briefly at

Hartung's treatment of the same phenomenon. Hartung
(1964:62) points out that there are many cases where
instead of a nominalization German permits the occurrence
of certain Demonstrative particles, which in traditional
grammar 'keinen festen Platz haben und teils als
beiordnende Konjunktionen, teils als Pronominaladverbien
betrachtet werden' (64). Having noticed that it is
necessary to state certain co-occurrence restrictions
for nominalizations but not for these Demonstrative
elements, Hartung proposes to derive the latter in a
different manner, which he refers to as
<u>Quasi-Nominalisierung</u>. He then continues:

> 'Es wäre natürlich denkbar, statt von einer
> Quasi-Nominalisierung von einer obligatorischen
> Pronominalisierung zu sprechen. Wir müssten dann
> die substantivische Nominalisierung in jedem
> Fall zulassen und dort, wo sich ungrammatische
> Konstruktionen ergeben, eine obligatorische
> Pronominalisierung folgen lassen. Die Zahl der
> Beschränkungen würde gleich bleiben, denn es
> ist dasselbe, ob wir die substantivische
> Nominalisierung beschränken oder zwischen
> fakultativer und obligatorischer Pronominalisierung
> unterscheiden. Aber abgesehen davon, dass die
> obligatorische Zerstörung einmal eingeführter

Einheiten ein unökonomischer Weg wäre, spricht
ein anderes Argument gegen die Annahme einer
Pronominalisierung: Jede Pronominalisierung
sollte die Vorerwähnung des zu pronominalisierenden
Gliedes voraussetzen' (63).

Hartung's objection to the pronominalization proposal
is justified only if (1) we operate in a framework
where constituent sentences start out as independent
structures rather than deep embeddings, (2) Hartung's
a priori, but nowhere justified, assumption about
pronominalization is accepted, and (3) elements
belonging to a discourse grammar are permitted to be
introduced into a single sentence grammar. Since in our
proposal embedded sentences start out in deep structure
as given, no need exists for stating the rather complex
embedding transformations and the associated constraints
on embeddings which Hartung has to state. Thus it is
not necessary to posit a nominalization place holder
which under certain conditions can be replaced by a
Demonstrative element.

Secondly, Hartung asserts that pronominalization
should presuppose a referent within the same simplex
or pair of adjoined simplexes. But consider the
following sentences:

(77)   Er weiss nicht, ob die Sonne morgen aufgeht.

(78)   Der Mann sitzt jeden Abend am Feuer.

Hartung does not show where the referent for the third
person anaphoric Pronoun of sentence (77) is to be
stated, if we limit ourselves to a single sentence.
By the same principle he would be obligated to show
where the referent for the definite Article in
<u>am Feuer</u> is stated.   I believe--as Jackendoff (1969),
e.g., has proposed for English--that pronouns may
have to be partly introduced in deep structure and
partly derived transformationally.   Thirdly,
Hartung assumes that such pairs as (79) and (80)

(79)   Der Kaufmann kündigte den Vertrag.

Deshalb blieben die Pferde im Stall stehen.

(80)   Der Kaufmann kündigte den Vertrag, weshalb
die Pferde im Stall stehen blieben.

have to be related.   It is not clear, however, that a
syntactic description which has a single sentence in
its scope--and that is certainly the most we can claim
to have accomplished--must relate these two alternatives.
Their parallelism is, of course, expressed in a
descriptively adequate grammar.   But this can be done
on the basis of identity of lexical items and tree

structures. It may even be argued that Hartung's
frequent attempt to relate two independent sentences
with structures where one of the sentences serves as
matrix sentence into which the other is embedded
represents a digression in term of our goal to
construct a sentence grammar, which must of necessity
separate out discourse considerations.

6.3.2. <u>Proform</u> <u>analysis</u>

I shall propose that the various Demonstrative elements
that substitute for the place holders in Hartung's
Quasi-Nominalisierungen are indeed proforms of lexical
head Nouns. Our lexical head Nouns are in principle
identical to what Hartung (1964:79) calls <u>abstract</u>
<u>Nouns</u>, which, as he observes correctly, may be
optionally realized on the surface. In addition to
the lexical head Noun itself the surface reflex may
also appear as a pronominal element, already demonstrated
in my discussion of the head Noun <u>Tatsache</u>; or there
may be no surface reflex whatsoever. This applies
not only to the Neutral case node but also to all other
case nodes for which arguments will be presented below.
Consider, e.g., the following parallel sentences, all
embedded under the Purpose node:

(81)   Der Verbrecher rasiert sich aus dem Grunde

        nicht, um nicht verkannt zu werden.

(82)   Der Verbrecher rasiert sich $\begin{Bmatrix} \text{deshalb} \\ \text{daher} \\ \text{darum} \end{Bmatrix}$ nicht,

        um nicht verkannt zu werden.

(83)   Der Verbrecher rasiert sich nicht, um

        nicht verkannt zu werden.

The lexical head Noun dem Grunde, depending on
the Purpose Preposition aus, is replaced in sentence (82)
by a number of proforms. In sentence (83) no surface
realization of the lexical head Noun appears. Hartung's
correct observation (1964:80) that certain abstract
Nouns--our lexical head Nouns--may occur without a
complement requires no further apparatus in my
description, since lexical head Nouns may, and usually
do have independent status as Nouns of the language.

Thus I am proposing that darum is one of a number
of proforms that can replace the Purpose head Noun
Grunde.[6] There is, however, no reason to assume that
the one is derived from the other. If the full lexical
head Noun is impossible in some cases it will be
obligatorily marked [+Pro]. The relationship between
lexical head Nouns and their proforms should not be
handled in the transformational (syntactic) component

at all. It seems that this type of information belongs
rather in the lexicon (cf. footnote (6)).

6.3.3. Additional support for lexical head and proform analysis

6.3.3.1. Determiner restrictions

My proposal, I believe, completely eliminates Hartung's
objection to the pronominalization analysis of
Demonstrative particles. It also accounts for the
fact that some Nouns can either occur as lexical
head Nouns or as independent Nouns without an
associated complement. This fact is particularly
important because of the restrictions on the choice
of Determiner. For example, the ungrammaticality of
(84b) versus the grammaticality of (85b)

(84a) Er lief aus dem Grunde weg, damit man
       seine Schandtaten nicht entdecken sollte.

(84b) *Er lief aus einem Grunde weg, damit ...

(85a) Er gab den Grund an.

(85b) Er gab einen Grund an.

is made explicit by the structure of the NP dominating
the Noun Grund in each case. Underlying (84a) is the
structure (T84a)

(T84a)

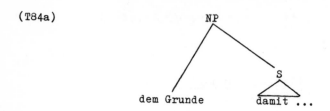

dem Grunde   damit ...

where the presence of the complement requires <u>Grund</u>
to take a definite article. In sentence (85b) the
structure is simply as illustrated in (T85b)

(T85b)

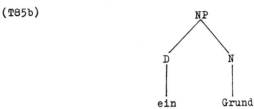

ein   Grund

where there is no restriction on the choice of Determiner
as one would expect. The analysis given here permits
us to account naturally for the syntactic differences
between Nouns in their function (1) as lexical heads
and (2) as independent Nouns.

6.3.3.2. <u>Constraints</u> <u>on</u> <u>topicalization</u>

Additional evidence for the lexical head analysis can
be derived from constraints on topicalization. Bierwisch
(1963:135) has observed that in certain cases it is
not possible to prepose single elements of a dependent
clause without fronting the entire clause. Yet he was

unable to explain this phenomenon. Notice, for example,
that die Unterlagen can be preposed in sentence (86)
but not in (87):

(86)   Die Unterlagen, bittet er dich, morgen
       mitzubringen.

(87) *Die Unterlagen, bittet er dich darum, morgen
       mitzubringen.

Similarly (88) and (89):

(88)   Den Mann, hofft er, nächstes Jahr
       wiederzusehen.

(89) *Den Mann, hofft er darauf, nächstes Jahr
       wiederzusehen.

If the Demonstrative particles darum, darauf, etc.-which
apparently prevent the splitting of dependent clauses-are
interpreted as proforms of lexical heads an explanation
of the facts is possible. Both the Kiparskys (1968)
and the UESP grammar (1968:2.577ff.) have observed
that Ross' Complex-NP-constraint applies only to NP's
with a lexical head. If no lexical head is present,
however, or if it has been deleted by the time the
constraint applies the movement transformations which
move elements out of an NP are not blocked.

Applying this criterion to sentences (86) - (89)

it becomes apparent that topicalization is blocked
only in those cases where a lexical head is present,
thus reflecting Ross' Complex-NP-constraint by blocking
movement across a lexical head.

The deep structures for (86) and (87) would then
be represented as (T86) and (T87) respectively:

(T86)

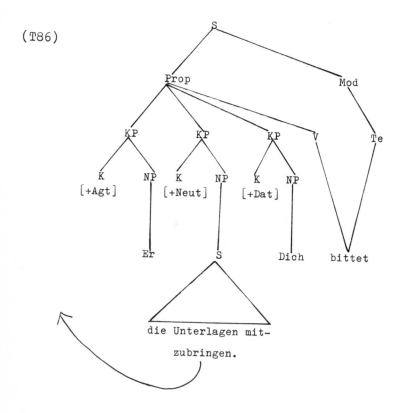

(T87)

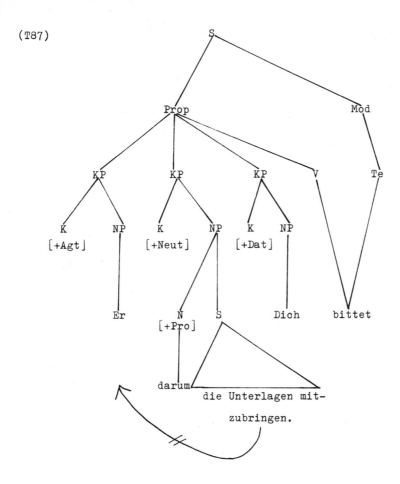

If <u>darum</u> is analyzed as a proform of a lexical head
Noun the topicalization constraint observed by Bierwisch
can be explained as a subcase of the presumably universal
Complex-NP-constraint formulated by Ross.

6.4. <u>Concluding</u> <u>remarks</u>

The concept <u>lexical</u> <u>head</u> will be of prime importance
in my description of complementation. The difference
between sentences (81), (82), and (83) above is then
a function of the various surface realizations of the
lexical head. Otherwise their tree structures and
lexical material are completely parallel. Since such
parallel groups of sentences (as (81) - (83)) are
extremely common in German, the <u>lexical</u> <u>head</u> analysis
provides us with a simple device to account for these
consistent parallels and differences in a natural
way.

7. DASS AND RELATED COMPLEMENTIZERS

In this section I treat a number of Complementizers, incorporating the notion of lexical head Nouns as propounded in chapter 6. An extremely thorough transformational analysis of complementation has recently been provided by Hartung (1964), who treats among many others also the five Complementizers to be investigated here: dass, damit, ob, um zu, and zu. It is my contention that the dass-complementizer is in some way the most basic of these Complementizers. For this reason I shall be primarily concerned with the dass-complementizer. The others, which occur either in complementary distribution with dass or as optional variants of dass, are of secondary interest only.

7.1. DASS complements under Purpose, Manner, Result, and Neutral

I intend to demonstrate that the Complementizer dass

or <u>so dass</u> can introduce complements embedded at four
different places in the deep structure phrase marker
(PM). In traditional grammars these notions have
in part been captured, for example, by such terms as
'Folgesätze', 'Gliedsätze ... die den Zweck des
Sachverhalts im Hauptsatz erklären', 'Subjektsätze',
'Objektsätze' oder 'der konsekutive Gliedsatz
[der sich] nicht auf den ganzen Sachverhalt im
Hauptsatz, sondern nur auf einen bestimmten Teil des
Sachverhaltes bezieht' (Schulz-Griesbach 1965:267, 270),
usually followed by a list of examples for each case.
The following examples demonstrate the various uses
of <u>dass</u>:

(1)   Der Junge stellt sich extra dumm, (so)
      dass seine Eltern ihn nicht in die höhere
      Schule schicken.

(2)   Der Lehrer gab dem Schüler das Buch, (so)
      dass er es bis zum nächsten Morgen lesen
      konnte.[1]

(3)   Er fuhr so schnell, dass er das Auto nicht
      mehr anhalten konnte.

(4)   Er benahm sich so, dass alle Leute anfingen,
      auf ihn aufmerksam zu werden.

(4') Er benahm sich, dass alle Leute anfingen,
      auf ihn aufmerksam zu werden.

(5) Als wir ankamen, war der letzte Zug schon

 abgefahren, so dass wir mit dem Taxi fahren

 mussten.

(6) Als er am späten Abend in Köln ankam, waren

 die Hotels schon alle besetzt, so dass er

 kein Zimmer mehr bekommen konnte.

 (Schulz-Griesbach 1965:270)

(7) Ich weiss, dass man sich beim Essen nicht

 auf den Ellbogen stützt.

(8) Er glaubt, dass ich nie verliebt gewesen bin.

The preceding sentences can be divided into four
groups according to the place where their
dass-complements are embedded:

(i) Sentences (1) and (2) are instances of

 embedding under the Purpose node;

(ii) The dass-clauses in (3), (4) and (4') are

 embedded under the Manner node;[2]

(iii) Sentences (5) and (6) contain dass-clauses

 that are embedded under a node which I shall

 tentatively refer to as Result and

(iv) the dass-clauses of sentences (7) and (8)

 are embedded under the Neutral node.

In the following section I shall justify my analysis.
First I illustrate the deep structures of the four

types of embeddings in the order: <u>Purpose</u>, <u>Manner</u>,
<u>Result</u>, and <u>Neutral</u>:

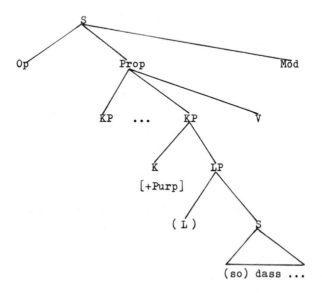

Fig (1): Embedding under Purpose

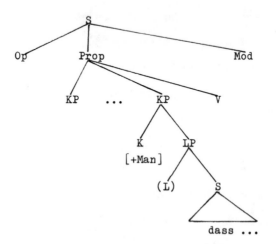

Fig (2): Embedding under Manner

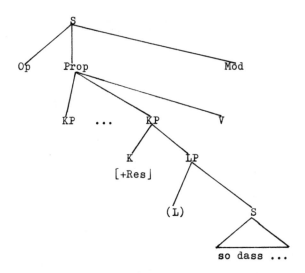

Fig (3): Embedding under Result

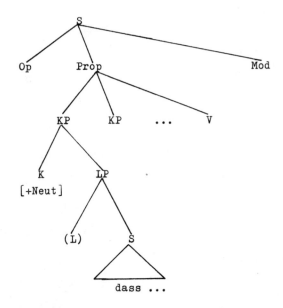

Fig (4): Embedding under Neutral

7.2. Justification for DASS-embeddings

7.2.1. Semantic argument

The first argument in support of my analysis is semantic. Every German speaker will without much difficulty separate out the various meanings. He may not be able to state exactly what the difference is, but he can tell clearly that there is a semantic distinction as indicated by the traditional labels listed above.

The clause dass ich nie verliebt gewesen bin in sentence (8) is perceived by all speakers as equivalent to das in (9):

(9)   Er glaubt das.

Thus if speaker A and B both knew that Hans is at home and speaker A would say Ich weiss, dass er zu Hause ist, speaker B would most likely answer Ich weiss das auch. Das is here without question a Neutral NP.

The interpretation of sentences (3) and (4) as embeddings under the Manner node can be more easily comprehended if we paraphrase the sentences by inserting derartig, dermassen, auf solche Art und Weise or something similar. Sentence (3) might then be rendered as (10):

(10)   Er fuhr derartig (schnell), dass er das Auto
nicht mehr anhalten konnte.

Also, the interpretation which places (1) and
(2) under the Purpose node is supported by inserting
<u>zu dem Zweck</u>. Thus sentence (2) can only be rendered
as (11)

(11)   Der Lehrer gab dem Schüler das Buch zu dem
Zweck, dass er es bis zum nächsten Morgen
lesen konnte.

where sentences (2) and (11) mean approximately the same.
Sentences (5) and (6) clearly differ from all
the rest by having a consequential relationship, i.e.,
the <u>dass</u>-clause is the result of the rest of the
sentence. This can again be demonstrated by inserting
a Result phrase; sentence (6) can, e.g., be paraphrased
as:

(12)   Als er am späten Abend in Köln ankam,
waren die Hotels schon alle besetzt. Die
Folge war, dass er kein Zimmer mehr
bekommen konnte.

7.2.2. Surface forms of Complementizers

A second reason for embedding dass-clauses under four
different nodes in the deep structure concerns the
surface realization of the Complementizers. If the
clause is embedded under the Purpose node, dass is the
normal form but the complement may also optionally
be realized as so dass.[3] The complement is always
dass (never so dass) in case of an embedding under
the Manner node. The same form dass is obligatory
in case the clause is embedded under the Neutral node.
And only with the Result interpretation, i.e., when
embedded under our tentative node Result must so dass
be obligatorily realized.

7.2.3. Distribution of related Complementizers

Next we shall be concerned with the distribution of
the other Complementizers mentioned: ob, damit, um zu
(zu will be treated later). Both damit and um zu
can occur when the clause is embedded under the Purpose
node. Damit is an optional variant of (so) dass.
It is preferred by many speakers as the better form
(as mentioned above).

7.2.3.1. UM ZU-Complementizer

Um zu, on the other hand, is the complement of both
damit and (so) dass, if the Subject of the complement
is identical to the Subject of the matrix sentence
and not realized in the surface structure. Consider
the following sentences:

(13) Er geht zur Schule, dass er etwas lernt.

(14) Er geht zur Schule, damit er etwas lernt.

(15) *Er geht zur Schule, um er etwas zu lernt.

(16) Er geht zur Schule, um etwas zu lernen.

Sentences (13) and (14) are semantically equivalent
as is sentence (16). In order to derive (16) besides
(13) the Subject of the dass-clause in (13) has to
be identical to the Subject in the main clause. If
the Subjects are not identical, the um-zu structure
is excluded, as in sentence (19).

(17) Er gibt seinem Sohn einen Ball, dass er
      spielen kann.

(18) Er gibt seinem Sohn einen Ball, damit er
      spielen kann.

(19) *Er gibt seinem Sohn einen Ball, um spielen
      zu können.

Sentence (18) might possibly be interpreted as:
'He$_i$ gives his son a ball, so that he$_i$ himself can
play'.

7.2.3.2. Leys' analysis of ZU and UM ZU

Leys (1971) has suggested that the Subject of an
um zu clause must not necessarily be identical to
the Subject of the matrix sentence. Correspondingly
Bech (1957:§364) has noticed that there exists a
small number of Verbs (senden, schicken, bringen, etc.)
where the identity condition can also hold between
the Subject of the um zu clause and the Object NP
of the matrix sentence if it is [+Animate]. But
even here the choice between the two animate NP's
is by no means optional as Leys apparently assumes.
Consider the sentences:

> (20) Der Mann gibt seinem Freund den Hund, um
>   ihn (den Freund) loszuwerden.
> (21) Der Mann gibt seinem Bruder das Geld, um
>   das Haus abzuzahlen.

In sentence (20) the identity condition holds between
Subject and Subject but in sentence (21) between
Object and Subject (actually sentence (21) is
ambiguous). Clear is that the Subject - Subject

identity condition can only be violated by a small
number of Verbs--for example, the Verbs of exchange
referred to in chapter 5. A detailed analysis of
um zu complementation with these Verbs is forthcoming.
I shall, therefore, say no more about this problem
here.

It should, however, be pointed out that the analysis
given by Leys can hardly be correct. Leys fails to
recognize that there are definite constraints on
both matrix and embedded Verbs which determine the
nature of the identity condition. This leads him
apparently to accept such sentences as:

(22) Die Mutter brachte das Kind zum Kindergarten,
      um besser spielen zu können (das Kind
      spielt!) [51]

I have been unable to find a native speaker for whom
this sentence was grammatical, without substituting
the damit Complementizer.

Moreover Leys extends this Equi-NP ambiguity to
other Verbs, as in the following sentences, which are
supposed to be grammatical:

(23) Der Wagen stand vor der Tür, um ihn zu
      polieren [45]

(24)   Die Kinder standen in einer Reihe, um sie zu
       zählen. [46]

Since much of Leys evidence is of similar quality, as
the above ungrammatical examples, his proposal can
be dismissed.

7.2.3.3.   Neutral DASS-embedding

The Neutral dass-clause is limited to a certain group
of Verbs and Adjectives and excluded from others. Among
the Verbs which can take the Neutral dass-complement
are the following:

  I.   antworten, bedauern, behaupten, beweisen,
       bewundern, empfehlen, entdecken, sich entschuldigen,
       erfahren, erkennen, erklären, erlauben, erwarten,
       fühlen, glauben, lesen, lügen, riechen, träumen,
       sagen, schmecken, schreiben, schreien, sehen,
       übersehen, vergessen, verhehlen, verheimlichen,
       verhindern, verstehen, vorgeben, sich vorstellen,
       vorziehen, widerrufen, wissen, zugeben.

The following group of Verbs does not, however, permit
a Neutral dass-clause:

 II.   anbinden, anfassen, arbeiten, aufschauen,
       bedienen, betasten, bewegen, bleiben, bringen,
       einpacken, erwachen, erziehen, fahren, fliegen,

füllen, geben, gehen, haben, hämmern, reiten,
schwimmen, sein, spielen, stehen, töten, umstossen,
umziehen, verreisen, wachsen, sich waschen, werfen.

Among Adjectives that permit a Neutral <u>dass</u>-complement
are the following:

III.   edel, ehrlich, entrüstet, erbärmlich, erlaubt,
       erstaunlich, erstaunt, erträglich, falsch,
       gewiss, grausam, interessant, nett, nötig,
       rätlich, schlecht, schön, sicher, sündhaft,
       süss, taktvoll, unerhört, unerlaubt, unerträglich,
       unglaublich, unhöflich, unmännlich, unmässig,
       unmöglich, unnütz, unverschämt, wunderbar,
       wütend, zufrieden.

The next group consists of Adjectives that do not permit
a Neutral <u>dass</u>-clause:

IV.   alt, dünn, eifrig, eingreifend, einträchtig,
      geheim, gesättigt, gesamt, gewöhnlich, gross,
      kalt, klein, krampfhaft, krank, kunstvoll,
      lang, laut, lose, machtvoll, matt, persönlich,
      streng, stumpf, unpässlich, unpolitisch,
      unsterblich, verliebt, verschieden, verspielt,
      vertraulich.

It is not entirely clear to me if a single feature

is common to the Verbs and Adjectives that permit a
Neutral dass-clause, a single feature that sets them
off from all other Verbs and Adjectives. Group I and
III are definitely more similar to each other
than either is to group II or IV.

I was unable to find another syntactic test
that would include all the forms of one of these groups
with the exclusion of the others. But there are a
number of sub-groupings in the various groups that
have similar membership classes. (See appendix.)

The conclusion seems to be that while the groups
function similarly in a number of syntactic environments,
no exact parallelism is apparent. This may indeed
indicate 'that all grammars leak'.

7.2.3.4. OB-Complementizer

Turning now to arguments concerning the other
Complementizers, we find that ob is in complementary
distribution with dass, when the dass-clause is embedded
under Neut. The ob-complementizer is limited to a
small group of Verbs and Adjectives. Consider the
following examples:

> (25) Er weiss, dass der Mensch irrt, solange er
>   strebt.

(26) *Er weiss, ob der Mensch irrt, solange er
     strebt.

(27) Weisst du, ob der Hahn gekräht hat?

(28) Er weiss nicht, dass der Hahn gekräht hat.

(29) Er weiss nicht, ob ...

(30) Ich habe vergessen, ob Novalis die blaue
     Blume je gefunden hat.

(31) Ich habe vergessen, dass ...

(32) *Ich habe nicht vergessen, ob ...

(33) Ich habe nicht vergessen, dass ...

(34) Ich erinnere mich daran, dass er das gestern
     gesagt hat.

(35) *Ich erinnere mich daran, ob ...

(36) Ich erinnere mich nicht daran, ob ...

(37) Ich erinnere mich nicht daran, dass ...

There are a few Verbs and Adjectives of knowing or
recognition which permit the ob-complementizer when
used with a negative. Among them are:

nicht wissen	nicht sicher
nicht verstehen	nicht gewiss
nicht erfahren	sich nicht erinnern an

Note that sentence (26) is ungrammatical since ob
cannot be used with these verbs in the indicative
unless Neg is in the tree. This fact is also confirmed

by such lexical items as <u>vergessen</u>, <u>ungewiss</u>, and
<u>unsicher</u> although superficially it does not appear that
way. <u>Ob</u> may be used with these forms when no negative
particle occurs in the sentence but not if Neg is
present (see sentences (30) and (32). To account for
this irregularity, we must assume a Neg in the deep
structure with these forms. This may indicate that
lexical formatives <u>vergessen</u>, <u>ungewiss</u>,etc. are
really combinations of Neg + <u>erinnern</u> and Neg + <u>gewiss</u>
which may optionally be introduced into the derivation
as <u>vergessen</u> and <u>ungewiss</u> respectively. We could then
account for the ungrammaticality of (32) but the
grammaticality of (36). If this analysis is correct,
sentences (30) and (36) should be semantically
equivalent, as indeed they are.

Some Verbs of inquiry require <u>ob</u> obligatorily
in all environments. Among these are <u>fragen</u>, <u>versuchen</u>,
<u>untersuchen</u>, <u>nachsehen</u>. Sentences (40) and (41) below
show the ungrammaticality of <u>dass</u> with these Verbs:

(38) Ich frage ihn heute, ob er Mundgeruch hat.
(39) Ich frage ihn nicht, ob er Mundgeruch hat.
(40) *Ich frage ihn heute, dass ...
(41) *Ich frage ihn nicht, dass ...

There are some Verbs of communication that allow <u>ob</u>

optionally in both positive and negative sentences, such as <u>mitteilen</u> and <u>sagen</u>.

Insertion of the Complementizer <u>ob</u> could be made dependent on the presence of the interrogative marker (Inter) in the complement. Thus sentence (29) could be derived from (42):

(42) $_S$[Neg er weiss $_{Neut}$[Inter der Hahn gekräht

hat]$_{Neut}$]$_S$

It should be noted that the inquiring nature of the Verb appears to trigger <u>ob</u> in the dependent clause, but this is only true for Verbs which obligatorily take <u>ob</u>. For the rest it is in part the Neg marker and in part some feature such as [+Communicative]. However, if the Inter marker is also present in the main clause of sentences such as (26), <u>ob</u> becomes possible in nonnegative contexts as well, as in (26'):[4]

(26') $_S$[Inter er weiss $_{Neut}$[Inter der Hahn gekräht

hat]$_{Neut}$]$_S$

There is some evidence indicating that perhaps the introduction of Inter into the complement is not

the correct analysis. We have, for example, such
sentences as:

> (43) Ich bin nicht sicher, ob er zu Hause ist
>   oder nicht.

For sentence (43) we must assume an underlying

> (44) Ich bin nicht sicher, ob er zu Hause ist
>   oder ob er nicht zu Hause ist.

My intuition is that both (43) and (44) should
be derived from the same deep structure as sentence (45):

> (45) Ich bin nicht sicher, ob er zu Hause ist.

The alternative <u>oder nicht</u> is also clearly implied in
(45). If only one part of the disjunction (i.e., positive
or negative) occurs in the DS then the <u>dass</u>-complement
is introduced, but if both the positive and the
negative alternative are in the DS the <u>ob</u>-complementizer
is chosen. In sentence (45) the second alternative
has been deleted. Sentence (43) preserves only the
Neg element of the second part of the disjunction,
which is the contrasting element between the two
alternatives. The rest is deleted.[5]

This analysis allows us (1) to relate sentences (43),
(44), and (45); (2) it shows that the real difference

between <u>ob</u> and <u>dass</u> is that <u>ob</u> presents a choice

between the positive and the negative alternative

whereas <u>dass</u> implies only one of these, and (3) the

interrogative marker is no longer necessary to trigger

the choice of Complementizers since <u>ob</u> and <u>dass</u> are

selected on the basis of whether one or both alternatives

occur in the complement.

There is also some counterevidence indicating that

perhaps the introduction of Inter for the purpose of

Complementizer selection is not the correct analysis.

Consider the following sentences:

(46a) Bist du sicher, ob er zu Hause ist?

(46b) *Du bist sicher, ob er zu Hause ist?

(46c) Du bist sicher, dass er zu Hause ist?

Sentence (46a) is only marginally grammatical for some

speakers of German. Nevertheless, since some speakers

do accept the <u>ob</u>-complementizer in this context, I

shall bring this evidence to bear on the final decision

concerning <u>ob</u>-complementation.[6]

Sentences (46b) and (c) are assertions intonated

as questions. The intonation pattern for sentence (46c)

may, therefore, be represented as follows:

(46c') Du bist sicher, dass er zu Hause ist?

If interrogation is realized by pitch as in (46b) rather
than by word order as in (46a), we notice that <u>ob</u>
becomes clearly ungrammatical. If the introduction of
<u>ob</u> were made dependent on the presence of the interrogat-
ive marker in the sentence, it would not be possible to
throw out sentence (46b) if the speaker should decide
to realize interrogation through pitch rather than
word order, which must be a relatively late rule of
the grammar. This fact points to the disjunction
analysis of <u>ob</u>-complementation which has been adopted
here rather than to one that employs the interrogative
marker as distinguishing element.

There are other examples parallel to (46a) which
are clearly grammatical. Consider, e.g., the sentences:

(47) Wir wissen, ob Heinrich heute **kommt** oder
      nicht, aber ihr wisst es nicht.

(48) Er wusste sehr wohl, ob er nach Italien
      fahren konnte oder nicht, aber seine Miene
      liess nichts davon erkennen.

Both sentences must be read with contrastive stress
in order to be acceptable. Thus the two highest
stress points in sentence (47) are on <u>wir</u> and <u>ihr</u>.
In sentence (48) they are on <u>wohl</u> and <u>Miene</u>. These
examples further support the disjunction analysis

of <u>ob</u>-complements. Sentence (47) would not be as
readily accepted by native speakers if the <u>oder nicht</u>
were deleted. This seems to indicate that in cases of
structural ambiguity the speaker will be less likely
to delete other syntactic clues that could help to
disambiguate the sentence. Thus in our case where
we would normally expect only the <u>dass</u>-complementizer
the speaker has a tendency to retain an additional clue
for the disjunctive structure of the <u>ob</u>-complement,
therewith signaling to the hearer, 'the <u>ob</u>-complement
is not a mistake but necessary to render the disjunctive
interpretation I want to convey to you'.

7.2.3.5. <u>Concluding remarks</u>

The discussion above has shown that the Complementizers
<u>dass</u>, <u>damit</u>, <u>um zu</u> and <u>ob</u> can be introduced
transformationally since it is possible to distinguish
among them on the basis of the structural description
of their associated complements. It has further become
apparent from the examples (46) - (48) that the
Complementizers may have to be introduced relatively
late in the derivation.

7.2.4. <u>Pronominalization argument</u>

The next argument makes use of the way in which the

various <u>dass</u>-complements pronominalize. Consider the following sentences:

(49)   Er gibt dem Jungen das Geld, damit er endlich Ruhe hat.

(50)   Er gibt ihm das Geld dafür.

(51)   Siegfried badet sich im Blut des Drachen, damit er rote Backen erhält.

(52)   Siegfried badet sich darum im Blut des Drachen.

(53)   Odin hing sich an den Baum, damit sich die Germanen endlich untereinander verständigen konnten.

(54)   Odin hing sich dazu an den Baum.

Sentences (49), (51), and (53) are cases of Purpose embeddings. Yet we notice that they are pronominalized in three different ways, with <u>darum</u>, <u>dafür</u>, and <u>dazu</u>.

Now let us look at the following sentences which represent cases of Neutral embeddings:

(55)   Der Mann glaubt, dass die Erde rund ist.

(56)   Der Mann glaubt es.

(57)   Dass der Zug zu spät ankommt, passiert nicht oft.

(58)   Es passiert nicht oft.

Es and das are the proforms for dass-clauses which are
embedded under the Neutral node, whether the dass-clause
is realized as surface Subject as in (57) or as surface
Object as in (55).

The next sentences contain cases of dass-embeddings
under the Manner node:

(59)   Er fuhr das Auto so schnell, dass er es
       nicht anhalten konnte.

(60)   Fuhr er das Auto derartig, dass er es nicht
       anhalten konnte?

the response might be (61) or (62):

(61)   Ja, er fuhr es so.

(62)   Ja, er fuhr es derartig.

Thus the proform for a dass-clause embedded under Manner
is so. Similarly, if one were to ask

(63)   Hat er es auf diese Weise gemacht?

it would be natural to answer

(64)   Ja, er hat es so gemacht.

So replaces the PP auf diese Weise which is here
considered a Manner case phrase. Therefore, so must
be assumed to be the proform for dass-clauses under

Manner. We have purposely not included Manner under
the Instrumental node, as is done, e.g., in the UESP
grammar for English. One of the reasons is that
Instrumental NP's are pronominalized with <u>damit</u> or
<u>dadurch</u>, whereas a Manner NP or clause has <u>so</u> as
proform. Consider, e.g.:

> (65) Ich habe das ganze Haus mit Kohlen geheizt.
> (66) Ich habe das ganze Haus damit geheizt.

The last type of <u>dass</u>-clause is the one which we
have embedded under the node Result. It stands all
by itself in that it does not have a proform. This
may indicate that this <u>dass</u>-complement is not embedded
in deep structure like the others but that we instead
have two originally separate sentences which are
related syntactically by the Complementizer <u>so dass</u>.
Consider again our sentence (5):

> (5)   Als wir ankamen, war der letzte Zug schon
>   abgefahren, so dass wir mit dem Taxi fahren
>   mussten.

It is obvious that the relation between the clause
introduced with <u>so dass</u> and the rest of the sentence
is much looser than in any of the other cases. The
notion <u>consequence</u>, which is really the only noticeable

tie between the two parts is also an inherent feature
of the Complementizer <u>so</u> <u>dass</u>. A certain degree of
consequence can be perceived in all other <u>dass</u>-clause
embeddings, although perhaps this is least perceptible
in the embedding under Neutral. It may be possible,
therefore, that <u>so</u> <u>dass</u> can relate two independently
derived sentences if the semantic notion of consequence
is to be expressed. The only syntactic consequence
is that the Complementizer <u>dass</u> induces subordinate
clause order in the clause it introduces. Which one
of these alternatives is correct will have to be
justified on empirical grounds.

7.2.5. <u>Proform</u> <u>argument</u>

One very common phenomenon in German is the frequent
anticipation of <u>dass</u>-clauses by the proform
<u>da</u> + Preposition, if the Verb is marked obligatorily
for a certain Preposition, e.g.:

> (67) Ich brauche den Hammer dazu, um den Nagel
> einzuschlagen.

This type of anticipating proform is particularly
common with Purpose clauses, occurring even if the
Verb does not normally take a Preposition as in:

(68)   Er hat es darum gemacht, damit du ihn
       endlich in Ruhe lässt.

The most frequent of these proforms (excluding the
case (67), where the form depends on the Preposition
of the Verb) are darum, dafür, dazu. These proforms
suggest strongly that there must be a separate Purpose
node and can be regarded as evidence for a lexical
head Noun in the Purpose complement. Otherwise we
would either have to assume a copying transformation
that would copy the Purpose clause and then be realized
as proform in the matrix sentence or posit a place
holder as is done by Hartung (1964).

   There is additional evidence for a lexical head
Noun under the Purpose node. Consider the following
sentences:

(69)   Der Mann erhielt das Brot zu dem Zweck, dass
       er seine Kinder damit ernähre.
(70)   Der Mann erhielt das Brot dazu, dass ...
(71)   Der Mann gab dem Jungen das Geld dafür, dass
       er seiner Mutter ein Geschenk kaufen konnte.
(72)   Der Mann gab dem Jungen das Geld für den
       Zweck, dass ...

Sentences (69) and (70) are semantically equivalent

and must be considered as coming from one DS. The
same is true for sentences (71) and (72). The PrepP's
<u>zu dem Zweck</u>, <u>für den Zweck</u>, <u>aus dem Grunde</u> are evidence
for a lexical head Noun under the Purpose node. This
head Noun can be realized in various forms and be
replaced by a corresponding proform or deleted
altogether as in (73):

(73)   Der Mann erhielt das Brot, damit ...

<u>Dazu</u> appears to be the proform for <u>zu dem Zweck</u>,
<u>dafür</u> the proform for <u>für diesen Zweck</u>. It is not
immediately obvious for which lexical head Noun <u>darum</u>
should be regarded as proform. The PrepP that
immediately comes to mind is <u>aus dem Grunde</u>. We would,
however, expect to find the Preposition <u>um</u> used with
the lexical head related to the proform <u>darum</u>. Although
there is no reason why the proform must have the same
Preposition as the lexical head Noun it replaces, this
is generally the case. The irregularity calls for an
explanation. I suggest that <u>darum</u> is a fossilized
form that served as proform for an archaic <u>um des Grundes</u>
<u>willen</u> or some similar expression which has become in
modern German <u>aus dem Grunde</u>.

As indicated earlier, there is also some evidence
for a lexical head Noun if the <u>dass</u>-complement is

embedded under the Neutral node. We have already
referred to the es-pronominalization of dass-clauses.
This es can also anticipate the dass-clause, without the
latter becoming deleted as in:

(74) Ich bereue, dass ich ihn gehen liess.

(75) Ich bereue es, dass ich ihn gehen liess.

Whether this es is the proform for die Tatsache, i.e.,
a Factive es--as was suggested above--or not is
irrelevant here. It does, however, indicate that a
lexical head Noun must be present in some cases of
Neutral dass-embeddings.

Justification for positing a lexical head Noun
under the Manner node can be derived from sentences
such as:

(76) Er hat ihn auf diese Weise zur Tür
       hinausgeschmissen.

(77) Die Frau fährt das Auto auf eine Weise,
       dass jede Woche etwas anderes kaputtgeht.

Sentences (76) and (77) can be restated as (78) and (79):

(78) Er hat ihn so zur Tür hinausgeschmissen.

(79) Die Frau fährt das Auto so, dass ...

The prepositional phrase auf diese Weise in sentences (76)
and (77) must be embedded under Manner. This explains

the proform <u>so</u> possible in both cases. Instead of
sentence (79) one can also get:

(80) Die Frau fährt das Auto, dass ...

Although the lexical head under the Manner node has
been deleted in this case, it is still clearly
understood by any speaker of German. The systematic
alternation <u>auf diese Weise</u>/<u>so</u>/∅ can again be easily
accounted for if a lexical head is assumed.

Another interesting phenomenon are pairs of
alternations, where in one sentence a proform is present,
while it is absent in the other. These pairs have at
times been interpreted as semantically equivalent.
In Schulz-Griesbach we read, e.g.,: 'Bei Verben,
die ein präpositionales Objekt verlangen,aber seelische
Vorgänge bezeichnen, können <u>da(r)</u>-und die Präposition
im Satzfeld fehlen, wenn ein Objektsatz mit <u>dass</u> im
Nachfeld steht' (267). This seems to imply that
the proform + Preposition can be optionally deleted.
I believe that this analysis is not correct. Consider,
e.g., the following sentences:

(81) Sie wartet, um ihn wiederzusehen.

(82) Sie wartet darauf, ihn wiederzusehen.

(83) Sie hofft, ihn wiederzusehen.

(84) Sie hofft darauf, ihn wiederzusehen.

The difference between (81) and (82) as well as between
(83) and (84) can be better shown by formulating
questions to which the above sentences could be answers:

    (85)   Worauf wartet sie?

    (86)   Auf was wartet sie?

    (87)   Warum wartet sie?

Sentence (81) can be the answer to question (87) but
not to the other two. Sentence (82), on the other
hand, can be taken as an answer to questions (86) and
(85) but not to (87). The distinction is even clearer
when lexical head Nouns are inserted into both (81)
and (82) to give sentences (88) and (89) respectively:

    (88) Sie wartet $\begin{Bmatrix} \text{aus dem Grunde} \\ \text{darum} \end{Bmatrix}$ $\begin{array}{l}\text{um ihn} \\ \text{, wiederzusehen.}\end{array}$

    (89) Sie wartet auf die Gelegenheit, ihn
                                          wiederzusehen.

Notice that in sentence (88) we can replace <u>um</u> <u>zu</u> with
the <u>damit</u>-complementizer, making the necessary changes,
but that this is impossible in sentence (89). We can
also construct a nominal form for (88) but not for
(89); thus we get:

    (90) Ihre Erwartung, ihn wiederzusehen ...

but not

(91)   *Ihre Erwartung darauf, ihn wiederzusehen ...

If the complement in sentence (88) is embedded under
the Purpose node with optional deletion of the lexical
head or its proform, but the complement in sentence (89)
under Neutral, also with an optional deletion of the
head Noun (whatever this might be) than all the facts
can be handled rather easily.

Sentences (83) and (84) also differ in some way,
but there it is not a difference in the place of
embedding. Sentence (83) can only be the answer to
question (92) and sentence (84) the answer to (93):

(92)   Wen hofft sie wiederzusehen?

(93)   Worauf hofft sie?

The Nominal alternative is again possible with sentence
(83) but not with (84). The difference between the two
sentences seems to be that in sentence (84) there is
a lexical head in the DS, also preserved as proform
on the surface, whereas in sentence (83) no such
lexical head Noun exists. The nominalized alternative
apparently is not possible under the Neutral node
if a lexical head Noun is present. Thus we get (94)
but not (95):

(94) Ihre Hoffnung, ihn wiederzusehen ...

(95) *Ihre Hoffnung darauf, ihn wiederzusehen ...

The same constraint may also be necessary for the Purpose
node--at least the proform cannot be present if we
nominalize. However, in some dialects of German
sentence (96) is considered grammatical

$$(96) \quad \text{Ihre Erwartung} \begin{Bmatrix} \text{in der Absicht} \\ \text{zu dem Zweck} \end{Bmatrix}, \quad \text{ihn wieder-} \\ \text{zusehen ...}$$

whereas sentence (97) is always ungrammatical:

(97) *Ihre Erwartung auf die Gelegenheit, ihn
        wiederzusehen ...

The constraints concerning the nominalized alternative
are not entirely clear and are only tentatively suggested
here. However, syntactic and semantic differences between
the alternating sentences differing only in the presence
of a proform clearly support the analysis of
dass-complementation presented above and show the need
for an optional lexical head Noun with the complement
expansion in the base.

In the case of the dass-complement which I have
introduced under Result, no evidence exists that a
lexical head Noun can be introduced into the matrix
sentence preceding it. This may suggest that the

second alternative for deriving Result <u>dass</u>-clauses
is preferable.

7.2.6. <u>Structure of Manner node</u>

Next I briefly sketch how I expect the Manner node to
be structured and how <u>dass</u>-complementation under the
Manner node fits in with the treatment of Adjectives
and Adverbs. Consider first sentence (98):

(98) Er singt so laut, dass ihn jeder hören kann.

Sentence (98) is clearly ambiguous between Manner and
Purpose interpretation. This fact is independent
evidence that we need to embed both under Manner and
Purpose nodes. We can, e.g., paraphrase the Manner
interpretation as (99):

(99) Er singt auf eine solch laute Weise, dass
      ihn jeder hört.

This interpretation does not allow the <u>dass</u>-complementizer
to be replaced by <u>damit</u>. Thus (100) is ungrammatical:

(100) *Er singt auf eine solch laute Weise, damit ...

However, if (98) is interpreted as a Purpose clause then
<u>damit</u> becomes possible, as is demonstrated by (101)

(101) Er singt so laut, damit ihn jeder hört.

which may be paraphrased as (102):

(102) Er singt zu dem Zweck so laut, damit ihn ...

Now consider the following sentences:

(103) Er schickt den Brief erst am 23ten ab, so

dass er vor Weihnachten nicht mehr ankommt.

(104) Der Junge schreit am lautesten, so dass seine

Mutter ihn aus dem Zimmer schickt.

(105) Er trinkt den Kaffee zu heiss, so dass er

sich die Zunge verbrennt.

All three sentences may be interpreted as containing
either Purpose complements or Result complements. In
all of them so dass can either be replaced by damit or
one can insert die Folge war. A Manner interpretation
is not possible in these cases.

7.2.6.1. Adjectives and Adverbs

I propose to introduce the various degrees which Adjective
and Adverbs can take under Adv which in turn is a
sub-node of the Manner node. I am not concerned at this
point with the exact form of the rules, but there will be
a rule of the following kind in our grammar:

$$\text{Adv} \longrightarrow \begin{cases} \text{Excessive} & \longrightarrow & \underline{\text{zu}} + (\text{Adj } \emptyset \text{ Adv}) \\ \text{Analogical}^7 & \longrightarrow & \underline{\text{so}} + (\text{Adj } \emptyset \text{ Adv}) \\ \text{Superlative} & \longrightarrow & \underline{\text{am}} + (\text{Adj } \emptyset \text{ Adv}) + \text{sten} \\ \text{Comparative} & \longrightarrow & (\text{Adj } \emptyset \text{ Adv}) + \text{er} \end{cases}$$

They would then be realized as:

Excessive	$\longrightarrow$	<u>zu</u> <u>laut</u>
Analogical	$\longrightarrow$	<u>so</u> <u>laut</u>
Superlative	$\longrightarrow$	<u>am</u> <u>lautesten</u>
Comparative	$\longrightarrow$	<u>lauter</u>

Only one of these alternatives can be chosen at each time. This explains why (106) and (107) are grammatical but (108) is not:

(106) Er fährt so schnell, dass ich ihn nicht einholen kann.

(107) Er fährt schneller, dass ich ihn nicht einholen kann.

(108) *Er fährt so schneller, dass ...[8]

But notice that both the Analogical and the Comparative are possible if one is embedded in the other:

(109) Er fährt so viel schneller, ...

The last example comes from a structure where <u>so viel</u>
is embedded under the Comparative node, i.e., <u>so viel</u>
<u>mehr schnell</u>.

Sentence (106) is ambiguous between Manner and
Purpose interpretation of the complement, whereas
(107) can only have a Purpose reading. This is,
however, explained by the fact that only the analogical
<u>so</u> can take both Manner and Purpose embeddings. The
other three permit only Purpose complements. Our
analysis accounts for these constraints in a very
natural way.

7.2.6.2. <u>Other</u> <u>parallel</u> <u>structures</u>

The introduction of the <u>dass</u>-complement requires moreover
much wider considerations than just the structure of
the Manner node. As Bowers (1970) has shown for English
(the same is also true to some degree for German) the
<u>dass</u>-complement under the Manner node is in some ways
parallel to the <u>als</u> or <u>wie</u>-complement under that
node with the Comparative and Analogical degree
respectively. The same structural parallelism can be
detected in relative clause insertion, so that parallels
extend to the various syntactic categories. To account
for the similarity of their internal structure I shall

make use of the earlier introduced X-Bar convention.
It will become apparent that the $\overline{X}$ convention is not
only applicable to express the similarity between
the internal structure of lexically derived Nominals
and sentences, but that it can be extended to Adjectives,
Adverbs, and even Determiners as well.

7.2.6.3. Incorporation of X-Bar convention

We shall now modify our rules from chapter 4 somewhat
to allow for the introduction of Adjectives and Adverbs
with their complements under the Manner node. Applying
the earlier introduced $\overline{X}$ convention to our base, rule 5
of chapter 4 can be rewritten as:

$$\text{Rule 5':} \quad \text{LP} \longrightarrow \left\{ \begin{array}{ll} \text{(L)} \quad\quad \text{S} & \text{a} \\ \text{Spec } \overline{\text{L}}, \overline{\text{L}} & \text{b} \end{array} \right.$$

where LP = $\overline{\overline{X}}$ and [Spec $\overline{\text{L}}$] $\overline{\text{L}}$ is equivalent to Chomsky's
[Spec $\overline{\text{X}}$] $\overline{\text{X}}$. The expansion (5b) is then a cover symbol
for Robinson's:

$$\text{LP} \longrightarrow \text{KP} \quad \text{L}.$$

The inversion KP   L is necessary since this leads to a
simpler description, as will become apparent. KP re
writes not only as NP, AdjP, and VP but also as AdvP. If

$\overline{L}$ = NOM then Spec $\overline{L}$ = Det, or to keep our terminology
constant DetP. Thus Spec $\overline{L}$ can be NP, VP, AdjP, AdvP
or DetP. L is rewritten as either NOM, V, Adj, Adv or
Det. If the next higher node is DetP, L will be
rewritten as Det. The expansion LP $\longrightarrow$ (L) + S,
therefore, introduces relative clauses into the Det
node, as has, e.g., been suggested by Chomsky (1967)
and Bowers (1970). This means that expansion (6a)
of chapter 4 is no longer needed. Rule 6 can now
be rewritten as:

> Rule 6': NOM $\longrightarrow$ N (((KP) (KP) ...) Mod).

LP may be rewritten as either AdjP or AdvP if it is
preceded by $\left[{}_{+Manner}^{K} \right]$, i.e., these occur only under
the Manner node.

The $\overline{X}$ convention gives us, therefore, the following
three parallel constructions under the cover expansions
(5a) and (5b):

$$(110) \begin{bmatrix} LP \longrightarrow & DetP & NOM \\ DetP \longrightarrow & Det & S \end{bmatrix}$$

(actually there would be an intermediate expansion:
LP $\longrightarrow$ KP NOM;

KP $\longrightarrow$ (K) DetP;

DetP $\longrightarrow$ (D) S.)

$$(111) \begin{bmatrix} LP \longrightarrow & AdjP & Adj \\ AdjP \longrightarrow & Adj & S \end{bmatrix}$$

$$(112) \begin{bmatrix} LP \longrightarrow & AdvP & Adv \\ AdvP \longrightarrow & Adv & S \end{bmatrix}$$

Figure (5) represents the structure produced by the above rules:

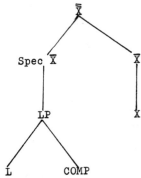

Fig (5): Tree structure produced by rule 5

The COMP element is introduced under [Spec, $\overline{X}$] and thus under either AdjP, AdvP,and what is here called DetP. These three categories show striking parallels in their internal structure, reflected by the number of transformations which apply to all three of them, justifying the above rule schema.

Bowers (1970) following Chomsky (1967) has demonstrated a number of parallels between the different categories. The same thing holds also true for German, which is the reason for my adoption of Bowers' scheme

in the description of complementation in German. I
shall not attempt a thorough analysis of the facts,
since Adjectives, Adverbs, and relativization is not
my primary concern. I feel, however, that my treatment
of <u>dass</u>-complements requires a decision on this matter
as well, so that I shall give a limited number of reasons
for adopting this particular analysis. Consider first the
similarity between Adjective and Adverbial constructions:

(113)   Er fährt so schnell, dass ich ihn nicht
        sehen kann.

(114)   Er ist so gross, dass er über den Tisch
        sehen kann.

The structure of the AdvP in (113) would be represented
as in Fig (6) using the base rules introduced earlier:

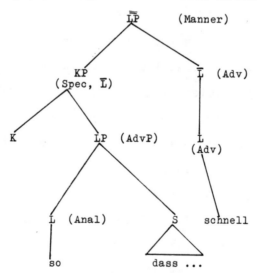

Fig (6): Tree diagram for the AdvP in sentence (113)

The AdjP in (114) would be represented as:

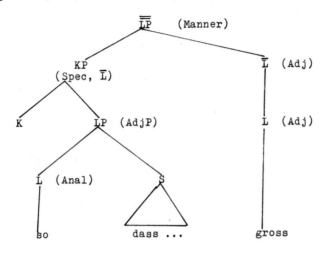

Fig (7):   Tree diagram for the AdjP in sentence (114)

Next consider a case of relativization as in the following sentence:

(115) Der Mann, der gestern zurückkam, ist mein Vater.

Our rules would give us the following structure for the Det node:

(T115)

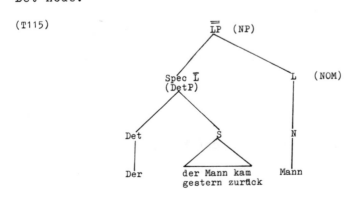

It is apparent that we need the same transformation
to move the complement in the AdvP in Fig (6), the
AdjP in Fig (7), and the DetP of (T115):

(116) $_{Man}[_{AdvP}[$so $_S[$dass ich ihn nicht sehen

kann$]_S]_{AdvP}$ schnell$]_{Man}$

(117) $_{Man}[_{AdjP}[$so $_S[$dass er über den Tisch sehen

kann$]_S]_{AdjP}$ gross$]_{Man}$

(118) $_{NP}[_{DetP}[$der $_S[$der Mann gestern zurückkam$]_S]_{Det}$

Mann$]_{NP}$

to derive the strings:

(116) .. so schnell, dass ich ihn nicht sehen kann.
(117) .. so gross, dass er über den Tisch sehen kann.
(118) .. der Mann, der (Mann) gestern zurückkam.[9]

I shall not present any more arguments for the use
of the $\bar{X}$ convention in these cases; there are clearly
other cases of parallelism in the way in which Adjectives
and Adverbials are moved as, e.g.:

(119a) So schnell lief der Mann, dass ihn der
Polizist nicht einholen konnte.

(119b) So gross ist der Junge, dass er schon auf den
Tisch sehen kann.

There are also parallels to the Adjectival so-dass
construction under the Manner node as in the sentence

(120) Er war grösser als der andere Junge (gross war)

which can be derived in the same way.

7.2.7. ZU-Complementizer

The last Complementizer considered in this section is
zu. Although zu appears to occur only in one environment
(often referred to as zu + infinitive) it is mistaken to
assume that all occurrences of a surface zu have the
same origin. Consider, e.g., the following pair of
sentences:

(121) Der Mann zwingt Tante Anna zu heiraten.
(122) Der Mann glaubt, Tante Anna zu heiraten.

These two sentences (similar to Chomsky's pair (a) he is
eager to please and (b) he is easy to please) have the
identical surface form, yet their underlying structure
is quite different. The difference can easily be seen
by applying certain transformations to strings (121)
and (122). E.g., string (121) can be passivized but
string (122) cannot:

(123) Tante Anna wird von dem Mann gezwungen zu
       heiraten.

(124) *Tante Anna wird von dem Mann geglaubt zu
       heiraten.

Note also that we can have the nominalized alternative of
sentence (121) but not of sentence (122):

(125) Der Mann zwingt Tante Anna zum Heiraten.

(126) *Der Mann glaubt Tante Anna zum Heiraten.

This indicates that the deep structures for sentences
(121) and (122) are not at all alike, as is illustrated
in (T121) and (T122) respectively:

(T121)

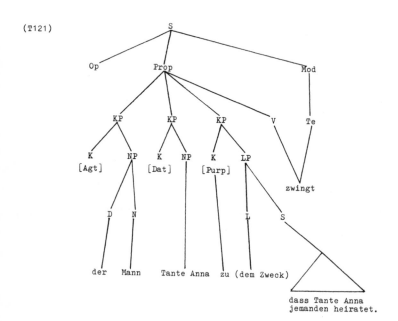

(T122)

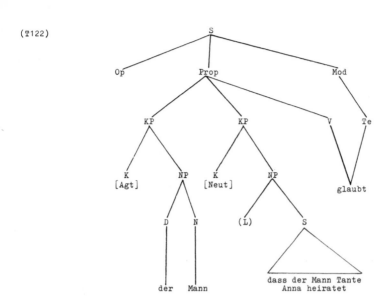

In order to account for sentences like

    (127)   Der Mann zwingt seinen Freund

we must assume <u>zwingen</u> to have a Dative in its case frame.
This means that two deletion transformations operate on
the structure (T121); an Equi-NP transformation deletes
the identical NP in the embedded S, which would in the
corresponding <u>dass</u>-clause become the Subject, as in (128):

    (128)   Der Mann zwingt Tante Anna, dass sie jemanden
           heiratet.

An indefinite NP deletion transformation deletes the
indefinite Object NP of the <u>dass</u>-clause. The introduction
of the <u>zu</u>-complementizer instead of the <u>dass</u> is then the
result of the deletion of the Subject, with which the
Verb agrees as to number and person. It is obvious
that sentence (121) and (128) are paraphrases of one
another and can be traced to the same DS. If we assume
that the Complementizer is introduced by transformation
then the general rules of the grammar will in one case
derive sentence (121) and in the other sentence (128).
Introduction of the <u>zu</u>-complementizer can be made
dependent on the absence of a Subject in the embedded
S with which the Verb can agree.[10] The Verb will be
realized as the unspecified infinitive and trigger
the introduction of the <u>zu</u>-complementizer. <u>Dass</u> (as
has been sufficiently shown above) always needs a
finite Verb form in the clause, or to state this
differently: a surface Subject must appear in the
<u>dass</u>-complement with which the Verb can agree.

Both <u>zu</u> and <u>um zu</u> thus are the result of a Purpose
complement. However, there are obvious limitations
on their occurrence. For example, we cannot get the
string

(129) *Der Mann zwingt Tante Anna um zu heiraten.

just as we cannot get (130)

(130) *Der Mann glaubt Tante Anna um zu heiraten.

with the same interpretation as in (122). But the
ungrammaticality of (129) is also predictable from the
fact that the deleted NP of the um zu-clause must be
identical to the surface Subject of the main clause;
otherwise the zu-complementizer is inserted.   In
sentence (121) the deleted Subject NP is identical
with the surface Object of the main clause and
requires, therefore, the introduction of zu only.

Sentence (122) is also the result of an Equi-NP
deletion. In this case the deleted Subject of the
dass-clause is identical to the surface Subject of
the main clause. Since the Subject has again been
removed leaving a non-finite form of the Verb behind
zu is introduced with the same transformation as in
sentence (121). Um zu is impossible in this environment
since it requires an embedding under the Purpose rather
than the Neutral node.

If both the zu and um zu Complementizers are
distinguished from the Neutral dass-complementizer by
where the complement is embedded, we can account for
the occurrence of the nominalized alternative in some
cases. Consider the sentences:

(131)   Der Mann kauft das Buch um zu lesen.

(132)   Der Mann kauft das Buch zum Lesen

(133)   Der Lehrer zwingt den Schüler zu lesen.

(134)   Der Lehrer zwingt den Schüler zum Lesen.

(135)   Der Student glaubt, dass er fliegt.

(136)   Der Student glaubt zu fliegen.

(137) *Der Student glaubt zum Fliegen.

The nominalized alternative for the zu-clause is only
possible if the complement is embedded under the Purpose
node, whether the zu or um zu would be realized in
the corresponding sentence. But notice that the
nominalized form is not possible in all cases as is
demonstrated by (138) and (139):

(138)   Er will ihm das Buch zum Lesen geben.

(139) *Er will ihn das Buch zum Lesen zwingen.

It seems that the difference is due to the NP in the
zu-clause in one case and its absence in the other.
I.e., the NP das Buch in sentence (138) is part of
the matrix sentence, the identical NP of the clause
having been deleted by Equi-NP transformation. In
sentence (139), on the other hand, das Buch is part
of the complement and thus prevents a nominalized
alternative. Notice also the following sentences:

(140)   Er zwingt seine Tochter zu essen.

(141)   Er zwingt seine Tochter zum Essen.

(142)   Er zwingt seine Tochter, das Brot zu essen.

(143)   *Er zwingt seine Tochter, das Brot zum Essen.

Thus there appears to be a constraint which prevents the
nominalized alternative to the zu-clause whenever the
complement contains an additional NP that would not be
deleted in the surface structure. The structural
difference of sentences (138) and (139) is made clear
in the following strings:

(144)   Er will ihm das Buch dazu geben, dass er es
        liest.

(145)   Er will ihn dazu zwingen, $\begin{cases} \text{das Buch zu lesen} \\ \text{dass er das Buch} \\ \qquad\qquad\text{liest} \end{cases}$

The introduction of the optional Purpose proform shows
the structure of the main clause more clearly. It also
supports our analysis that these zu-clauses are embedded
under the Purpose node and are optional variants of
the dass-complement.

The zu-complementizer thus is the result of two
embeddings: under Neutral and under Purpose. This
analysis of the zu-complementizer has the advantage of
relating one source of zu with um zu by the position

of the embedded S while at the same time accounting
for the semantically identical sentence with a
dass-complementizer. There is then no need to ever
delete one Complementizer and replace it by one of the
others. If this analysis is correct, Complementizer
insertion is a relatively late rule in the grammar.

7.3. Transformational insertion of Complementizers

The basic contention underlying my description of
complementation has been (1) that the Complementizers
discussed in this section are best introduced
transformationally and (2) that the dass Complementizer
is the key to a description of the Complementizers
concerned. Since the syntactic environment for the
introduction of the Complementizers can be stated
unequivocally, there is no need to assume that
Complementizers are lexically introduced in the deep
structure. Moreover, the frequent ambiguity of surface
complements is best explained as the result of
different transformational paths.

8. Conclusions

The two areas of German syntax that have been
investigated in this study are nominalization and
complementation. My analysis of nominalization has

largely confined itself to two classes of Nominals: ung-nominals and infinitive Nouns. Although a transformational derivation would seem desirable at first--particularly for the infinitival Nouns--I have shown that this is not feasible for syntactic and semantic reasons. I have, therefore, proposed to derive both ung and infinitival Nouns lexically.

A careful analysis of the two Noun classes has further shown that they have a specific function within the lexicon of the speaker-hearer which can be identified with the Perfective and Durative Noun function. When the interrelationship among lexical classes is taken into account, ung-nominalization can be shown to be an active process in the language that is predictable from the presence or absence of other Nouns in the lexicon with the same function.

I have not attempted to establish any other lexical functions. However, the systematic interrelationship among members of the lexicon investigated can be assumed to extend to other parts of the lexicon as well. If it is true--as I have suggested earlier--that the language tends to prevent the occurrence of homolexons, so that we can in general expect one particular lexical form to fill each existing slot, then it should be

possible to determine the functional classes for the
total lexicon, which may be regarded as a finite and
bounded set.

My analysis of complementation has been limited
to five Complementizers. A comparison of the syntactic
environments has shown that they are in complementary
distribution. This suggests that Complementizers are
to be introduced transformationally since the structural
description for the insertion of a particular
Complementizer can be stated very easily. A
transformational insertion of these Complementizers is,
of course, preferable since (a) it expresses the fact
that the occurrence of a particular Complementizer can
be predicted from its surrounding syntactic environment
and (b) it expresses the generality of the process
much better than lexical insertion at the deep structure
level.

The functional parallelism between certain
Demonstrative particles and sequences of Preposition +
Demonstrative + Noun has long been realized as peculiar
to German.
Yet how to capture this parallelism in a syntactic description has always caused difficulty. The introduction
of an optional lexical head in the complement expansion,
which may be realized on the surface as either PrepP

or proform, offers a natural way to account for this
functional parallelism.

   The case model has provided us with a framework
that permits an adequate description of nominalization
and complementation in German. Although my description
has aimed at being a syntactic one, I have at the
same time aligned it as much as possible with deep
semantic (functional) relationships, in order to account
for the interaction of semantic and syntactic phenomena.
In this respect I have extended Fillmore's case
relations to the lexicon, to make possible the
description of the existing systematic interrelationships
between lexical formatives arising from the functional
structure of the lexicon.

Footnotes to Chapter 1

[1]This term has been used by Chomsky himself in
Chomsky (1969).

[2]Transformational rules, on the other hand, are
context sensitive; i.e., they include information
about the derivational history of its input strings.

[3]Tree diagrams which illustrate the structure of
a sentence under discussion carry the same number as
the corresponding sentence preceded by the letter T
in parenthesis. Thus, (T5) refers to the tree
diagram corresponding to sentence (5). Diagrams and
illustrations without corresponding sentences are
numbered independently, as Fig (1), (2), etc.

[4]The argument in this paragraph and the examples
in (9) have been adopted from the 'UCLA English Syntax
Project' henceforth referred to as UESP grammar
(1968:1.3 ff.).

[5]The authors of the UESP grammar have first critically examined the X-Bar convention. Their treatment is so thorough that the next two sections represent largely a restatement of ideas first expressed in the UESP grammar.

[6]In German, where only proper nouns are genitivized and preposed (cf. sentence (15b) in which the Agent phrase does not prepose), the parellelism between (15a) and (b) would even be less apparent than in the corresponding English structures.

[7]The author is fully aware of the problems with the case proposal, particularly as pertaining to the definitions of the cases themselves. Some of these have been discussed by Gruber (1965 and 1967), Stephen R. Anderson (1971), Huddleston (1970), Chapin (1972) and others. However, such deficiencies are to be expected at this stage in case research and do not detract from the over-all attractiveness of the model.

[8]This head-complement distinction has also been incorporated into the case model, in a less adequate way, I feel, by the UESP grammar.

Footnotes to chapter 2

[1]Cf. particularly McCawley (1968), (1970), and G. Lakoff (1966) and (1969).

[2]I am fully aware of the present division among scholars on this question. Arguments for the position that German is an SVO language will be considered below.

[3]For a discussion of Bach's (1971) SVO proposal, which is based on (1) Ross' gapping evidence and (2) universal constraints on question word movement, see Esau (1971b). I have demonstrated there that, even if Bach's universal constraint on question word movement is correct, no evidence has been presented that would support an SVO analysis for German.

Theo Vennemann also has recently accepted the SVO position. His reasons for positing SVO as the basic word order pattern in German are of a different kind. Beginning with an extremely abstract treatment of German phonology in 1968, Vennemann is now arguing for a very concrete linguistic description. His present position is that syntactic generalizations such as regular word order changes in a language are of little value in a grammatical description. It would be very hard to counter such basic objections

in the space available here, since it is based on
a different form of the linguistic model. I hope to
respond to this problem in a separate paper.

Footnotes to chapter 3

[1]This should not be taken to imply that there
do not exist any universal order principles. See,
e.g., Maling (1971) who has proposed a universal
principle that an underlying Dative + Neutral order
is the rule for languages of the SOV type, as I have
shown German to be.

[2]See, for example, Behagel's <u>Deutsche Syntax</u>
(608 ff.) for a discussion of the different kinds of
Datives.

[3]It should be mentioned that <u>zu</u> is only one of
a set of Locative Prepositions, whereas <u>für</u> is the
underlying Benefactive marker.

[4]This sentence has, of course, another reading
which is grammatical.

[5]This observation is not new. A similar analysis
can, for example, be found in Renate Steinitz,
<u>Adverbial-Syntax</u> (=<u>Studia Grammatica</u> X.)

[6]The sequence <u>tat dasselbe</u> substitutes for the
second occurrence of the VP <u>kaufte ein Haus</u>.

[7]Apparent exceptions to this rule are only the
Verbs which have an obligatory Locative or Temporal
complement, thus stative Verbs which logically do
not permit certain case phrases such as Instrumental.

[8]See Edmondson and Esau, <u>A</u> <u>functional</u> <u>theory</u> <u>of</u>
<u>the</u> <u>lexicon</u>, forthcoming.

[9]We will disregard the fact that both are cyclical
rules. It must be kept in mind, however, that the
order posited here, holds only for transformations
occurring in the same cycle.

Footnotes to chapter 4

[1]Emmon Bach has come to similar conclusions in
Bach (1969). See also J. G. Kooij (1971:94 ff.) for
an interesting discussion of Tense ambiguity. Kooij
has proposed to leave 'the nominalization itself ...
unspecified for "Tense"' (98). Instead he permits
every Nominal to be interpreted with respect to
(i) the <u>Time</u> <u>spoken</u> <u>about</u> (i.e., the Tense of the
sentence) and (ii) the <u>Time</u> <u>spoken</u> <u>at</u> (i.e., the
discourse in which it is realized).

[2]Note that the UESP grammar also uses such an
intervening NOM node.

[3]Cf., e.g., <u>Der</u> <u>Sprach-Brockhaus</u>[7] (Wiesbaden 1964).

[4]These constraints are stated in Hartung (1964:55 ff.).

[5]In a forthcoming paper I will show that possess-
ives--in contrast to Isacenko's argument (1964)--must
be derived from underlying Datives or Agentives and not
the other way around.

[6]Chomsky was the first to suggest such an object
fronting transformation for English in 'Remarks on
Nominalization'.

Footnotes to chapter 5

[1]I am not concerned here with whether the name
Perfective is the correct description of the Aspect
inherent in ung-nominals. Whatever this property,
it is shared by all Nominals of this class.

[2]I am fully aware of the parallelism with tagmemics
at this point, although I have been led into this
direction independently, partly as a consequence of
my having adopted Fillmore's case functions and partly
because the evidence seemed to require such an analysis.

[3]I.e., the speaker views the action or event with
the end-point in mind.

[4]Der Empfang is not the Perfective Nominal
corresponding to bekommen. Although there is some
overlapping between empfangen and bekommen, they are
not interchangeable.

[5]Even if the relationship between a Verb and
both Perfective Nominal forms is still recognizable,
it is generally the case that there is a significant
semantic distance between the Verb and at least one
of the two Nominal forms. Two Perfective Nominals

will rarely have an identical range of meaning
(semantic field), so that it should in general be
possible to identify that Nominal form which is
semantically closest to the corresponding Verb.

[6]The speaker will probably perceive both Vorsicht
and Vorsehung as related to the Verb vorsehen. However,
there must be two Verb entries vorsehen to account
for the following pair:

   (i) Er hat die Geburtstagsfeier für morgen
       vorgesehen.

  (ii) Er hat sich vor dem Auto vorgesehen.

Vorsehung is the Nominal equivalent to vorsehen in the
first sentence and Vorsicht corresponds to sich vorsehen
in the second sentence. Thus the alternation
Vorsicht/Vorsehung too will present no problem.

[7]I.e., that position of autonomous syntax which
disallows any form of semantic conditioning, as e.g.,
Chomsky's early view.

[8]Thus it would be possible to make the same threefold
division in syntax that has been proposed for phonology
between (1) existing, (2) possible but non-existing, and
(3) impossible forms.

[9]Notice that I am not claiming that the infinitive
Nominal can be either Durative or Perfective. Although
historically both interpretations of Leben are formed
with the same infinitival suffix en, synchronically
it is a coincidence that both interpretations have
merged into one form.

[10]Almost every description of nis-nouns indicates
that there are two classes, one group with Feminine
gender and a smaller group with Neuter gender. Yet
it seems that the gender of these Nouns is predictable
if one assumes the distinction [+/-Stative] for them.
Nis-nouns which are marked [+Stative] as Erkenntnis,
Wildnis, Finsternis, and Bitternis take a Feminine
gender but those marked [-Stative] as Verlöbnis,
Bekenntnis, Verständnis, Hindernis, Gefängnis take
a Neuter gender.

Footnotes to chapter 6

[1]Notice incidentally that cleft and pseudocleft
in English are used primarily for the purpose of
topicalization. This is, of course, due to the strict
<u>X Subject Verb</u> order. In German, on the other hand,
topicalization is done by permutation transformations.
Since German can make most any element topic of the
sentence by placing it in front of the Verb, the need
for the more clumsy topicalization procedure through
cleft or pseudocleft does not arise, so that it can
remain relatively unutilized. This may explain, why
clefting in German sounds somewhat awkward and
unnatural, whereas in English it leads to quite
acceptable surface strings.

[2]Cf., e.g., the argument concerning the
extraposition of the expletive <u>it</u>, which is probably
the weakest argument of all.

[3]The Factive/Nonfactive distinction has proven
to be an important dichotomy in discourse analysis,
particularly as a determinant of the presuppositional
content of compliment structures. Cf. especially
Lauri Karttunen (1971a), (1971b), and (1973) for a
discussion of factivity in this context.

[4]There are, of course, some syntactic restrictions
as well, but these it would be rather difficult to
state. Consider these sentences:

(1a) *Ich glaube, dass sie nach Hause komme.

(1b) Er glaubt, dass sie nach Hause komme.

(2a) *Ich sage, dass er Geld habe.

(2b) Er sagt, dass sie Geld habe.

(3a) *Wir sagen, dass der Zug nicht abfahre.

(3b) Sie sagen, dass der Zug nicht abfahre.

The subjunctive cannot occur if the main Verb in the
matrix sentence is in the first person singular or
plural of the present tense. This is not surprising,
since these are really cases of indirect discourse.
It is only to be expected that a speaker repeating
what has just been said in indirect speech would have
to use the past tense as in sentence (4), in which
case the subjunctive becomes grammatical:

(4)   <u>Ich sagte, dass er kein Geld habe.</u>

Thus this syntactic restriction is much deeper, and
not really a restriction on the subjunctive, but
rather due to the logical impossibility of retelling
one's own words indirectly in any other tense but
the past.

Such sentences as (5)

(5) <u>Das können sein</u>.

could be additional evidence for this phenomenon.
Perhaps sentence (5) should be derived from something
like (6):

<u>Ich glaube</u>, [<u>das kann sein</u> + Sbj]

where the speaker optionally deletes the [<u>ich glaube</u>]
if he wants to convey the additional semantic content
of uncertainty, made explicit on the surface by the
subjunctive. Then we could allow the deletion of the
matrix Subject and Verb in case it is in first person
of the present tense and the feature [-Certainty]
triggering the subjunctive is in the tree. This would
make it unnecessary to build in any other syntactic
constraints.

[5]The Kiparskys have claimed that the English Verb
<u>expect</u> is also neutral with regard to factivity so
that one can get both:

(1) I expected that there would be a big turnout ..
and
(2) I expected it, that there would be a big
turnout ...

The second sentence, however, is ungrammatical for almost
all English speakers I questioned. I suspect that
the latter sentence is a Germanism.

[6]It is interesting in this connection to notice
that the archaic Dative ending e is preserved in the
lexical head Noun Grund whereas it has virtually
disappeared in Nouns that do not function as lexical
heads as consistently as Grund does. This fact as
well as the frequent fossilization particularly of
proforms (infolgedessen, meinetwegen, währenddessen,
deswegen, in Anbetracht dessen, aus diesem Grunde)
points to the conclusion that the derivation of these
forms from independent minimal functional units does
not belong into the transformational component of a
synchronic grammar. Of course, it is interesting to
note existing regularities, but these should rather
be expressed in the lexicon.

Although such forms, as the ones cited above,
could frequently be broken down into sequences of
Preposition + Demonstrative or Preposition + Demonstrative + Noun, etc.--due to their particular historical
development--they function as lexical units which
the speaker manipulates as one whole and not as a
number of component parts. The lexicon is clearly

not without structure--as I have also shown in chapter 5--and such structural regularity, as can be determined, should be part of the description of the lexicon.

Footnotes to chapter 7

[1]Some speakers will prefer the use of <u>damit</u> instead
of <u>dass</u> or <u>so dass</u> for these examples. But there are
only few that would completely disallow the use of
<u>dass</u> in a Purpose clause. Since my grammar attempts
to describe the use of complementation for the normal
speaker of German, I shall disregard here the overly
sophisticated speaker who disallows <u>dass</u> in this
context altogether.

[2]The <u>dass</u>-clauses which I have embedded under
Manner have been listed under a variety of names such
as <u>degree</u> <u>clauses</u>, <u>extent</u> <u>clauses</u>, etc. I am less
concerned with the name of the node as I am to show
that all clauses embedded under it share a number
of properties that can only be adequately described
by making reference to such a node.

[3]For simplicity of description it will probably
be preferable to treat <u>so dass</u> as the basic Complementizer in this case and delete <u>so</u> optionally.

[4]Notice that it is again the [+/-Certainty]
distinction that is important for the introduction of
the <u>ob</u>-complementizer. Verbs like <u>wissen</u>, <u>gewiss</u>,

sicher, etc. share the feature [+Certainty]. In posi

tive contexts they can only take the dass-complementizer.

But if the Verb or Adjective marked for [+Certainty]

is negated or questioned--i.e., if in the context of

the entire sentence the [+Certainty] feature of the

Verb is converted into [-Certainty]--the ob-complementizer

is possible. This indicates that the [+/-Certainty]

distinction is an important one for the speaker of

German since it has a number of syntactic consequences;

it further supports my subjunctive and modal analysis.

[5]The analysis of ob-clauses given here corresponds

closely to Ross' sluicing analysis in Ross (1969).

Although Ross is arguing against a strawman, his

solution is quite convincing and the deletion analysis

of ob presented here may be regarded as one sub-case

of his sluicing proposal.

[6]In those dialects where sentence (46a) is grammatical

it is obviously a Mischform. The uncertainty of the

question apparently is stronger than the [+Certainty]

feature of the Verb, thus allowing the ob-complementizer

to occur with sicher.

[7]Some grammars call this equative.

[8]This constraint was pointed out to me by Mervin Barnes (personal communication).

[9]No movement is necessary, on the other hand, if the relative clause is realized as the extended participial construction:

Der gestern zurückgekommehe Mann ...

[10]This analysis was first suggested by Kiparsky.

REFERENCES

Bach, Emmon., 1962. 'The order of elements in a
    transformational grammar of German'. Lg 38, 263-69.
_____, 1969. 'Nouns and noun phrases'. In Emmon Bach
    and Robert T. Harms (eds.), Universals in linguistic
    theory, 91-122. New York, Holt, Rinehart and
    Winston, Inc.

Baumgärtner, Klaus, 1967. 'Forschungsbericht "Syntax
    and Semantik"'. Deutschunterricht für Ausländer
    17, 49-67.

Bech, G., 1955-57. Studien über das deutsche Verbum
    Infinitum. København, Det Kongel. Danske Vidensk.
    Selsk.

Bechert, Johannes, Danièle Clément, Wolfgang Thümmel
    and Karl Heinz Wagner, 1970. Einführung in die
    generative Transformationsgrammatik. München,
    Hueber Verlag.

Behagel, Otto von, 1923-32. Deutsche Syntax: Eine
    geschichtliche Darstellung. 4 Vols. Heidelberg,
    Carl Winters Universitätsbuchhandlung.

Bierwisch, Manfred, 1963. 'Grammatik des deutschen
    Verbs'. Studia Grammatica 2. Berlin, Akademie-Verlag
_____, 1967. 'Some semantic universals in German
    adjectivals'. Foundations of Language 3, 1-36.

Bierwisch, Manfred, 1970. 'Review of Hans Glinz,
       1965. Grundbegriffe und Methoden inhaltsbezogener
       Text- und Sprachanalyse'. Foundations of Language 6,
       284-96.

Bowers, John, 1970. 'Adjectives and adverbs in English'.
       Unpublished paper. Cambridge, Mass., M.I.T.

Brinkmann, Hennig, 1962. Die deutsche Sprache: Gestalt
       und Leistung. Vol. I. Düsseldorf, Pädagogischer
       Verlag Schwann.

Chomsky, Noam, 1957. Syntactic structures. The Hague,
       Mouton.

————————, 1965. Aspects of the theory of syntax.
       Cambridge, Mass., M.I.T.

————————, 1967. 'Remarks on nominalization'. In: Jacobs
       and Rosenbaum (eds.), 1970. Readings in English
       transformational grammar. Waltham, Mass., Ginn
       and Comp.

————————, 1969. 'Deep structure, surface structure, and
       semantic interpretation'. In: L. Jakobovits and
       D. Steinberg (eds.), Semantics: an interdisciplinary
       reader. Urbana, Illinois, University of Illinois Pres

————————, 1970. 'Some empirical issues in the theory of
       transformational grammar'. Unpublished paper.
       Cambridge, Mass., M.I.T.

Curme, George O., 1922[2]. A grammar of the German
    language. New York, Ungar.

Drach, Erich, 1940[3]. Grundgedanken der deutschen
    Satzlehre. Frankfurt, Diesterweg Verlag.

Droescher, W. O., 1969. 'German verb types'. Lingua
    24, 19-32.

Der Grosse Duden, 1959. Vol. IV: Grammatik der
    deutschen Gegenwartssprache, ed. by Paul Grebe et al.
    Mannheim, Dudenverlag.

_____, 1965. Vol. IX: Hauptschwierigkeiten der
    deutschen Sprache, ed. by Günther Drosdowski et al.
    Mannheim, Dudenverlag.

Esau, Helmut, 1972.   'A new approach to the teaching
    of word order in elementary German'. Die Unter-
    richtspraxis 5.127-39.

_____, 1971b. 'Some facts about German nominalization'.
    Neophilologus 55.150-56.

_____, 1971c. 'Order of the elements in the German
    verb constellation'. Linguistics 98. 20-40.

Fillmore, Charles J., 1968. 'The case for case'. In:
    Bach and Harms (eds.), Universals in linguistic
    theory. New York, Holt, Rinehart, and Winston.

Glinz, Hans, 1952. <u>Die</u> <u>innere</u> <u>Form</u> <u>des</u> <u>Deutschen</u>: <u>Eine</u>
neue deutsche <u>Grammatik</u>. Bern, Francke Verlag.

_____, 1965a. <u>Deutsche</u> <u>Syntax</u>. (In: Abteilung
Deutsche Sprachwissenschaft). Stuttgart, J. B.
Metzlersche Verlagsbuchhandlung.

_____, 1965b. <u>Grundbegriffe</u> <u>und</u> <u>Methoden</u>
<u>inhaltsbezogener</u> <u>Text-</u> <u>und</u> <u>Sprachanalyse</u>.
Düsseldorf, Schwann.

Gruber, Jeffrey, 1965. 'Studies in lexical relations'.
Unpublished doctoral dissertation. Cambridge,
Mass., M.I.T.

Hartung, Wolfdietrich, 1962. 'Die Passivtransformationen
im Deutschen'. <u>Studia</u> <u>Grammatica</u> 1. Berlin,
Akademie Verlag.

_____, 1964. 'Die zusammengesetzten Sätze des
Deutschen'. <u>Studia</u> <u>Grammatica</u> 4. Berlin, Akademie
Verlag.

Heidolph, Karl Erich, 1970. 'Zur Bedeutung negativer
Sätze'. In: Bierwisch and Heidolph (eds.), <u>Progress</u>
<u>in</u> <u>Linguistics</u>. The Hague, Mouton.

Helbig, G., 1965. 'Der Begriff der Valenz als Mittel der
strukturellen Sprachbeschreibung des
Fremdsprachenunterrichtes'. <u>Deutsch</u> <u>als</u>
<u>Fremdsprache</u> 2.10-23.

_____, 1966. 'Untersuchungen zur Valenz und Distribution deutscher Verben'. <u>Deutsch als Fremdsprache</u> 3.1-11.

Huddleston, Rodney, 1970. 'Some remarks on case grammar'. <u>Linguistic Inquiry</u> 1.501-11.

Isačenko, Alexander V., 1965. 'Das syntaktische Verhältnis der Bezeichnungen von Körperteilen im Deutschen'. <u>Studia Grammatica</u> 5. Berlin, Akademie Verlag, 7-27.

Jackendoff, R. S., 1969. 'Some rules of semantic interpretation for English'. Unpublished doctoral dissertation. M.I.T.

_____, 1972. Semantic interpretation in generative grammar. Cambridge, Mass., M.I.T. Press.

Karttunen, Lauri, 1971a. 'Discourse referents'. Mimeographed.

_____, 1971b. 'The logic of English predicate complement constructions. Mimeographed.

_____, 1973. 'Remarks on presupposition'. Xeroxed copy.

Katz, J. and P. Postal, 1964. <u>An integrated theory of linguistic description</u>. Cambridge, Mass., M.I.T. Press.

Kiparsky, P. and C. Kiparsky, 1968. 'Fact'. In: Bierwisch and Heidolph (eds.), 1970. <u>Progress in</u>

linguistics, The Hague, Mouton.

Lakoff, George, 1966. 'Deep and surface grammar'.

Unpublished paper. Harvard University.

_____, 1969. 'On generative semantics'.

In: L. Jakobovits and D. Steinberg (eds.), Semantics:
an interdisciplinary reader, Urbana, Illinois,
University of Illinois Press.

Lakoff, Robin T., 1969. Abstract syntax and Latin
complementation. Cambridge, Mass., M.I.T. Press.

Langacker, Ronald, 1970. 'Review of Spanish case and
function, by Mark Goldin'. Lg 46.167-85.

Lees, R. B., 1960. The grammar of English nominalizations.
The Hague, Mouton.

Leys, O., 1971. 'Die Präpositionalinfinitive im
Deutschen'. Leuvense Bijdragen 60.1-56.

Maling, Joan M., 1970. 'On "Gapping and the order of
constituents"'. M.I.T. Quarterly Progress Report
97.135-43.

McCawley, James D., 1968. 'The role of semantics in
grammar'. In: Bach and Harms (eds.), Universals
in linguistic theory. New York, Holt, Rinehart,
and Winston.

_____, 1970. 'Where do noun phrases come from'.
In: Jacobs and Rosenbaum (eds.), Readings in

English transformational grammar. Waltham, Mass.,
Ginn and Co.

Menzel, Peter, 1969. 'Propositions, events, and actions
in the syntax of complementation'. Unpublished
Ph.D. dissertation, UCLA.

Motsch,Wolfgang, 1964. 'Syntax des deutschen Adjektivs'.
Studia Grammatica 3. Berlin, Akademie Verlag.

Regula, Moritz, 1968. Kurzgefasste erklärende Satzkunde
des Neuhochdeutschen. Bern, Francke Verlag.

Robinson, Jane J., 1970. 'Case, category, and
configuration'. Journal of Linguistics 6.57-80.

Rosenbaum, Peter S., 1967. The grammar of English
predicate complement constructions. Cambridge,
Mass., M.I.T. Press.

Ross, John R., 1967a. 'Auxiliaries as main verbs'.
In: W. Todd (ed.), 1969. Studies in Philosophical
Linguistics. Evanston, Ill., Great Expectations.

————, 1967b. 'Constraints on variables in syntax'.
Unpublished Ph.D. dissertation, M.I.T.

————, 1969. 'Guess who?' Papers from the fifth
regional meeting of the Chicago Linguistic Society.
Chicago, pp. 252-86.

————, 1970. 'Gapping and the order of constituents'.
In: Bierwisch and Heidolph (eds.), Progress in
linguistics. The Hague, Mouton.

Schulz, Dora and Heinz Griesbach, 1965[3]. Grammatik der
    deutschen Sprache. München, Max Hueber Verlag.

Seuren, Pieter, 1969. Operators and nucleus: a con-
    tribution to the theory of grammar. (Cambridge
    Studies in Linguistics 2). Cambridge, University
    Press.

Steger, Hugo (ed.), 1970. Vorschläge für eine Struk-
    turelle Grammatik des Deutschen. Darmstadt,
    Wissenschaftliche Buchgesellschaft.

Tesnière, L., 1959. Eléments de syntaxe structurale.
    Paris, Klincksieck.

U.E.S.P., 1968. Stockwell, R. P., P. S. Schachter, and
    B. H. Partee, Integration of transformational
    theories on English syntax. 2 Vols. Govt.
    Document ESD- TR-68-419, Los Angeles.

Vendler, Z., 1968. Adjectives and nominalizations. The
    Hague, Mouton.

Weinreich, Uriel, 1966. 'Explorations in semantic
    theory'. In: Thomas A. Sebeok (ed.), Current
    trends in linguistics, Vol. III. The Hague, Mouton.

Wunderlich, Dieter, 1971. Warum die Darstellung von
    Nominalisierungen problematisch bleibt. (=Linguis-
    tische Reihe 8.) München, Hueber Verlag.

Appendix

The following Verbs in group I fit into the syntactic frame

$$\text{Ich} \left\{ \begin{array}{l} \text{weiss} \\ \text{glaube} \\ \text{bedaure} \end{array} \right\} \text{, er kommt.}$$

thus permitting the optional deletion of the dass-complementizer:

> antworten, bedauern, behaupten, erfahren,
> erklären, fühlen, glauben, lesen, sagen,
> sehen, träumen, vergessen, verstehen,
> vorgeben, sich vorstellen, vorziehen,
> zugeben.

On the other hand, this optional deletion is not possible with the following Verbs:

$$^{*}\text{Ich} \left\{ \begin{array}{l} \text{erkenne} \\ \text{verhindere} \\ \text{bewundere} \\ \text{beweise} \\ \text{erwarte} \end{array} \right\} \text{, er kommt.}$$

We obtain almost the same split if the nominalization
test is applied. Thus forms that do not permit the
optional complementizer deletion do take a nominalization
as complement:

$$
\text{Ich} \left\{ \begin{array}{l} \text{beweise} \\ \text{bewundere} \\ \text{empfehle} \\ \text{erlaube} \\ \text{erwarte} \\ \text{etc.} \end{array} \right\} \quad \text{sein Kommen;}
$$

But forms that do allow the optional complementizer
deletion transformation resist being used in this
syntactic frame:

$$
^{*}\text{Ich} \left\{ \begin{array}{l} \text{weiss} \\ \text{glaube} \\ \text{behaupte} \\ \text{antworte} \\ \cdot \\ \cdot \\ \cdot \end{array} \right\} \quad \text{sein Kommen.}
$$

The correspondence is, however, not entirely regular;
a few forms of the latter group also permit a
nominalization in the following complement as in:

$$\text{Ich} \begin{Bmatrix} \text{entdecke} \\ \text{gebe ... zu} \end{Bmatrix} \text{sein Kommen.}$$

If we compare the properties of the Verb forms in group I with those in group II we note immediately that almost all Verbs are <u>Verbs that semantically represent interior subjective experiences and decisions</u>. The imperative test shows--as one would expect--that for most of these Verbs an imperative would be semantically odd. Thus it would not make much sense to say:

$$? \begin{Bmatrix} \text{Wissen Sie} \\ \text{Träumen Sie} \\ \text{Vergessen Sie} \end{Bmatrix}, \text{dass Nixon der amerikanische Präsident ist!}$$

Most imperatives that are possible are only pseudo-imperatives, as can be seen if the Verbs are used in the frame <u>Ich befehle dir, dass</u> ... Consider, e.g.:

$$?\text{Ich befehle dir} \begin{Bmatrix} \text{zu riechen, dass der Kuchen} \\ \text{verbrannt ist.} \\ \text{zu hören, dass das Radio knackert.} \\ \text{dir vorzustellen, dass du Geld hast.} \end{Bmatrix}$$

Many of these Verbs will be accepted, however, if we use
a pseudo-imperative frame such as <u>Ich bitte dich, dass</u> ..
This is not surprising considering the nature of the
Verbs. Thus we get:

$$\text{Ich bitte dich} \left\{ \begin{array}{l} \text{zu glauben, dass} \\ \text{zu sagen, dass} \\ \text{zu verstehen, dass} \end{array} \right\} \dots$$

The Verbs of group II are clearly different in that
they can all be used naturally in the imperative frame
<u>Ich befehle dir, dass</u> ...

$$\text{Ich befehle dir,} \left\{ \begin{array}{l} \text{dass du gehst.} \\ \text{dass du das Auto fährst.} \\ \text{dass du mit ihm spielst.} \\ \text{dass du das Glas bringst.} \end{array} \right\}$$

All the Verbs in this group describe physical actions
and thus permit introduction into the imperative frame.
The Modals <u>haben</u> and <u>sein</u> do not fit with the rest of the
group, which indicates--what we would expect
independently--that they are in this group accidentally.

In order to permit neutral <u>dass</u>-clauses only with
the Verbs of group I they are marked with the feature
[+mnemotic]. The Verbs of group II will then be marked
minus that feature. <u>Mnemotic</u> is defined as the property
of Verbs, that with the action or state either a voluntary

mental decision is associated or that no such a decision
is possible, i.e., that property 'which represents
interior subjective experiences and decisions'.

The application of a number of syntactic tests to
Adjectives (groups III and IV) again showed certain
sub-groupings, but an exact correspondence of membership
classes was not always the case. E.g., the Adjectives
in group III will split the same way for the frame

Es ist $\{\quad\}$, dass ... as for the frame

Sein Kommen ist $\{\quad\}$.

The following forms are ungrammatical for each
frame. (I list the ungrammatical forms since there
are fewer of them):

$$^*\text{Es ist} \begin{Bmatrix} \text{zufrieden} \\ \text{wütend} \\ \text{erstaunt} \\ \text{entrüstet} \\ \text{ehrlich} \end{Bmatrix}, \text{dass} \ldots$$

and

$$^*\text{Sein Kommen ist} \begin{Bmatrix} \text{zufrieden} \\ \text{wütend} \\ \text{entrüstet} \\ \text{erstaunt} \\ \text{ehrlich} \end{Bmatrix}$$

But we get

$$\text{Es ist} \begin{Bmatrix} \text{grausam} \\ \text{schön} \\ \text{gewiss} \\ \text{unverschämt} \\ \cdot \\ \cdot \\ \cdot \end{Bmatrix}, \text{dass} \ldots$$

and

$$\text{Sein Kommen ist} \begin{Bmatrix} \text{grausam} \\ \text{nett} \\ \text{gewiss} \end{Bmatrix}.$$

The Adjectives of group IV do not generally fit into this frame, whereas the majority of group III does. I have not found another syntactic frame that results in the same distribution.

The Adjectives in group III and IV do not divide as nicely as do the Verbs. Many of the Adjectives of group IV are physical properties, whereas those of group III are in general properties that express an evaluation of the affecting Agent or the affected being or thing.

INDEX